to **MENTORS** everywhere - *we are better together*

Thoughts
Taking One Day at a Time

Capturing Courage Press is the publishing division
of Capturing Courage International.

capturingcourage.org
cyndy@capturingcourage.org

Capturing Courage Press
capturingcouragepress.org
publishing@capturingcouragepress.org

cyndylavoie.com
cyndy@cyndylavoie.com

book design | **tImmyroland**.com
cover photography | **shutterstock**.com

ISBN: 978.1.4675.5678.1

Contents

Thoughts

TAKING ONE DAY AT A TIME

by Cyndy Lavoie

CAPTURING COURAGE PRESS

Foreword

The first time I met Cyndy Lavoie I knew there was something special about her; she has a graceful presence that emanates her love of God and humanity. Every morning for the past year I have eagerly checked my email to be inspired by the "thought of the day" and I am simply delighted that they are available for all in print form.

The book that you hold in your hand is an outpouring of what is close to her heart: not just a collection of her daily thoughts but a series of careful meditations within the soul. Each page presents an encouraging and insightful glimpse into Cyndy's personal journey of discovery.

Many of these ideas are forward-thinking and challenge the very nature of our lifestyle. With life's ever increasing speed, these thoughts act as a gentle prompt for us to dedicate time just to think. It is in these rare moments of processing that we often realize what matters most to us, and then recognize that we've been completely preoccupied with something less important.

I have known Cyndy for a few years now, and every time we meet she just makes me want to be a better person. After reading this book, I'm sure you will feel the same.

Lynn Matson
Consultant

Introduction

This book was written almost by accident, yet entirely with purpose, a process of one step at a time, writing day by day, week by week over the course of a year and voila.

Life is exactly like this.

From day to day we barely see the progress, hardly comprehending any change from where we were to where we want to be. Yet, as we invest in each day, we look back and find that there has indeed been progress, and we are indeed farther along than we thought.

Thoughts - Taking One Day at a Time, is an investment in your future. I am privileged and honored to walk alongside your journey in this small way. I trust these thoughts and the heart behind them, make a difference for you.

Be encouraged, be challenged, go after growth, and fine-tune your life day by day. Most of all, make your life what you want it to be. With much grace and peace over you today.

Cyndy Lavoie

TAKING ONE DAY AT A TIME

January

JANUARY 1

The question uppermost in people's minds are,

How am I doing?

Does anybody care about me?

If there is a team, a family or an organization that you are part of, and if there is something not quite right, listen to your gut and then advocate for yourself around these questions.

Thoughts

JANUARY 2

The top quality of a leader is vision.

Having a picture of the future, a destination so to speak for your life, your organization or your family, is the key to advancing through life.

Without a focal point off on the horizon, we get overwhelmed by the rocks on the road, the pot-holes, and the ditches at our side

Keeping the picture of what you want, where you are going, and what you are heading towards is the single most important criteria of making things happen.

Thoughts

JANUARY 3

Listening is one of the most important skills we can grow, for listening is never automatic.

We in and of ourselves are far too invested in our filters and paradigms to really listen, without a lot of work and intention.

Invest in intentional listening, and set yourself apart from the crowd.

JANUARY 4

As influencers, it is our responsibility to 'learn the language' of those around us.

We can't claim ignorance, or put-off responsibility. If we were in another country, with a language we didn't know, we would be forced to use a lot more skills in our listening.

Every day we have opportunity to be fully present to another's 'speaking', making note of the non-verbal cues, right where we are.

Thoughts

JANUARY 5

Values are the core of a person or organization,
and the best values are clear, clean and inspiring.

Leaders deploy strengths in themselves and others,
and the way this happens is through a base-line grid
of values and the things that are most important
to you. Values are the non-negotiable of our core.

We all have them. It's important to know what they
are for they drive us more than we think.

What you value determines the DNA of your life,
your organization and how you interact and present
to the world.

Today, identify a non-negotiable of your own, then
articulate it into a value (a positive statement).

Thoughts

TAKING ONE DAY / AT A TIME

JANUARY 6

Gearing into another year is a great time for setting intentions and expectations.

Yet the most important thing, is to increase our bias towards action.

Having great ideas isn't good enough. It is follow-through and action that makes a difference.

How might you increase your bias for action today?

JANUARY 7

The ability to advance through life requires flexibility of heart and mind.

One of the greatest way to increase our internal flexibility is to grieve. There are a great many things around us that are not okay.

Delving deep into the emotions of what is not okay, opens up our worlds, our hearts and minds, to vast expanses of all that is good and right and powerful in our lives and our world.

JANUARY 8

Where do you put your creative moments?

How do you fit visioning and forecasting into
your week or month?

Every business, every life, requires time set aside
for taking stock. For the person who regularly makes
time for assessing and visioning is the one better
equipped to recognize opportunity and open doors,
taking advantage of timeliness each step of the way.

Thoughts

JANUARY 9

Twenty years ago it was quite possible to set five, ten, even twenty-five year goals, and methodically walk them out.

Today, in our new world of rapid transmission of ideas and collaborations, we must hold our goals loosely, and become better at adaptation and flexibility in the midst of walking them out.

Part of resilience in our new economy and way of doing business and life is this flexibility and adaptability.

Setting aside regular time to take stock of your goals, making spaces for creative responses, and you will find yourself effective and relevant in the face of changes yet to come.

JANUARY 10

It is counter-intuitive that through the power
of grieving we come to find the power of celebration
and delight. Yet this is a key aspect of increasing
flexibility of heart and mind.

So make sure to leave some space and time and
energy to grieve what is not okay. Then fasten your
seat-belt for the ride of your life as you experience
powerful celebration.

We just can't have one without the other.

JANUARY 11

There are times in our lives when one foot has stretched out into the new. When we've declared what we are going after, and with great intention we take a step forward.

What comes unexpected, is the span of time between the first leg engaging this stride and the second leg following along. For in that span of time, it seems that all is hanging in the balance.

Our natural human reaction is to shrink back from the discomfort, and to perhaps even shrink back from the stride taken. We wonder, "Am I doing the right thing?" Hang in there.

The natural momentum established by your step forward, will in fact reverberate through your being, your other leg will follow, and you will be on solid ground. You will wonder what you were ever worried about.

Thoughts

TAKING ONE DAY AT A TIME

JANUARY 12

There is a universal law that what we sow
is what we reap.

Simply this: Sow one seed of corn into the ground,
harvest a hundred-fold of corn seeds.

How it applies: Sow one seed of love, respect,
honor, good-will, excellence, benefit of the doubt,
peace, and reap a hundred-fold of the same.

Sow one seed of suspicion, pettiness, fear,
mediocrity, judgment, disregard, hatred, reap
a hundred-fold of the same.

What have you been sowing?

Thoughts

JANUARY 13

The most important task of a leader is to think.

Strategically moving forward requires keen thinking first and foremost. For the quality of our lives are dependent on the quality of our thinking.

And the best way to increase the quality of our thinking, is to build around us a grand assortment of thinkers.

Hang out with those whose thinking challenges you. It's outside our comfort zone we are grown.

JANUARY 14

Try personifying money. Take money and think
of it like a person. Now, listen real close to what
you have to say about this person.

You might hear things like, 'Money is dirty', 'I don't
care about money', 'There are more important things
than money', and so on.

Think about it, if we replaced 'money' with Mom,
or Joe, or Sally or Aunt Beth, how much would any
one of these want to hang out with us?

If you could use more money in your life, double
check your attitudes about it. You just might be
making your own trouble.

JANUARY 15

We are either creating or consuming.

We are either making money or spending money.

We are designed to create.

And if we are not tapped into the full expression
of who we are to be in the world, it is as though
we fill that space and that void with spending
and obviously, consuming.

Investing rather, all of who you are, living from the
core of your unique gifts to the world, will eliminate
the need to consume, and will do away with habits
of spending.

You will be making your own magic, from
the inside out, and nothing compares to the
satisfaction this brings.

JANUARY 16 2014

There are always rocks that show up on the paths
of our lives. Some of them, in fact, are more like
boulders. Boulders have the power to shut down
even the best of intentions. But should they?
Who gives them this authority?

Simply speaking, those who keep their eye on the
finish point, beyond the view of the boulder, are those
who reach their goals.

Keep your eye on the prize.

It is there for the taking.

JANUARY 17

Just before the crest of the hill it is darkest before
the dawn. That place where all our efforts and time
and energy could easily go either way, the way of
disaster or the way of triumph.

Perhaps you are here today, in some way, with
everything hanging precariously in the balance.

These are the times that we just keep going.

Because the hill will be crested, the horizon will
open before us, and the vista will prove itself
spectacular. One foot in front of the other, and the
mountain . . . it will be taken.

JANUARY 18

Fog obscures our journey. And like children we may be afraid of going forward. After all, we can't see the way. But unlike children, we know that once we walk forward into the fog, we can see.

Today's question, 'What fog-laden hill are you afraid to descend?' No matter, take heart, once you get there, you'll see just fine.

Vision comes to those who are moving forward.

Thoughts

JANUARY 19

It doesn't matter the life we have lived. At any given moment in time we can harness all of our experiences and the wisdom learned and invest these things for others.

Taking the best and the worst of our lives and leveraging it for another's benefit brings satisfaction hardly imagined.

Getting out of our own heads, and beyond our own realities, brings unstoppable influence.

You can make a difference today.

JANUARY 20

Jack be nimble, Jack be quick, Jack jump over the candlestick. Moving forward through this particular time in history, life is exponentially shifting and changing right before our eyes. Have you noticed?

Those who will be most successful are those who are nimble, who can act quickly and boldly, taking advantage of doors that are open, before they close. It's not about frenetic activity or haphazard guesses. Rather, that with doors opening and closing, we are simply ready.

JANUARY 21

A friend once pointed out, 'We marry according
to our self-esteem'.

Instantly knowing this to be true, we might ask,
'How has this impacted your life or the lives
of your friends?'

It is not a far leap to observe that our friends
reflect our self esteem as well. So, too our clients,
our colleagues, and closest associates.

For a moment consider: what do they tell you
about your self esteem?

JANUARY 22

How often do you take a personal day?

You know the kind with solitude of thought, space of being, and freedom to drink in the day.

A personal day gives a renewed grounding to who and what we want to be in the world.

Becoming re-acquainted with our strength, reminded of what matters most, and refreshed in body, heart, and mind, makes a personal day more of a necessity than a luxury.

JANUARY 23

If you want to get somewhere, gather people around you
who will encourage and advise, care for and take
a vested interest in your passions and dreams.

Nothing happens without a team, and creating
a team that is for you is a gift you give yourself.

It doesn't have to be a bit team, those on
it may change and shift over time, nonetheless,
once you have experienced the gift that a caring
group around you brings, you won't go back to
doing life on your own.

Thoughts

TAKING ONE DAY / AT A TIME

JANUARY 24

Build your community. Become deliberate about gather about you individuals that bring various viewpoints and expertise that is different than your own.

At the same time, gathering those who have similar values and understand the way we think and why we do the things we do.

The biggest risk: the internal process of becoming comfortable with sharing ourselves, speaking our passions, and becoming deliberate about life and community.

Take a chance and invest in community.

JANUARY 25

There are two disciplines of effective focusing.

One: the ability to engage sustained energy and thought towards one conclusion. With unswerving focus aimed at a particular result, success becomes ours.

Two: eradicating from our life and line of vision, all distractions.

Getting to our tomorrows means focussing even more. The further we walk towards our personal and integral successes, it becomes about putting aside really good things.

Let's go for the great.

Thoughts

TAKING ONE DAY / AT A TIME

JANUARY 26

Being naked is a powerful place to come from.

It's the place where we have nothing to prove.
Where there are no agenda's to fill and where
confidence naturally and simply becomes
a part of who we are.

The authenticity and transparency of nakedness
transforms every part of our lives.

Get a little more naked today.

JANUARY 27

The only thing that takes us forward through
the tough times is a strong vision.

It is why it has been said that without vision
a people perish.

Vision is more than goals. It is the end result,
the picture of what we are working towards.

A full vision encompasses touch, taste, sight,
smell, and emotions. Settle yourself into your vision.
What does it feel like? What do you see?

Tell me about the emotions.

Who are you in this place?

JANUARY 28

False humility does a number on all of us at one time or another. False humility keeps us from correct assessment of our gifts and talents, those special things that you bring to the world that none can duplicate.

The other name for false humility is pride.

We are all familiar with pride that puts us in the spot-light, but what about the pride that keeps us from living the best each of us can be

The kind of pride that masquerades as, 'Oh no, I'm not really that special.'

JANUARY 29

Each of us has an internal rhythmic setting in terms of work versus rest and task versus creative.

It is important to know your own rhythm, to work with it, and not against it.

Shooting upstream, going against the tide, pushing details when it is time to ponder, extracting results when it is time to rest, and vice-versa is not a long term plan.

While we all have to do this once in a while, a life spent out of sync with ourselves is not sustainable.

Live out the congruency of your own rhythms.

Internally you will have what you need for great works to come.

JANUARY 30

Success breeds success.

The question, 'How does one teach a rambunctious, conquer the world, three-year old boy to play quietly on his bed for an hour each day?' One minute at a time.

Outside his door, one minute . . . two minutes . . . three minutes . . . , 'Wow, you did fabulous!'

Next day 5 minutes. Next day 8 minutes.

You get the picture. Success in small increments sets the stage for more success, and then more, and then some more.

Something we are wise to do for others at all times, and just as important, a gift we can give ourselves.

Thoughts

JANUARY 31

Any change we want to make in our lives requires that we have a support base of others around us.

As people, we are meant to do life in community and in the company of others.

The bigger the work, the more people gathered.

Your own personal energy and focus invested in deliberate change, multiplies when joined with the energy and focus of those who simply know you and are for you.

That thing you are dreaming to do?

What kind of people do you need around you?

February

TAKING ONE DAY AT A TIME

FEBRUARY 1

Simply ask yourself, 'How might I?'
Then listen for the answer.

Trust it.

Put some action to it.

You will be exponentially closer to your own
great work than you will ever really know.

'How might I . . . ?'

FEBRUARY 2

Blowing past red lights is a dangerous way to live.

But not only on the roads. How many times
have you blown past 'red lights' in your business
or your relationships?

The things is, red flags are often subtle. They show
up as lots of little things going wrong.

They are indirect, speaking a language of suggestions
and questions, and it is easy to pay them no mind.
Until after the fact.

Pay attention to your red flags, they are
telling you something.

Thoughts

FEBRUARY 3

Starting something new is scary.

Starting something new brings us back to novice, beginner, and amateur.

None of which are nice things especially once we've gotten used to seasoned, confident, and expert.

Going back to the beginning where we know less than we knew before, doesn't make a lot of sense.

Unless, we want to achieve more than we've ever achieved before.

Unless we want to bring to the world something we've never brought before.

FEBRUARY 4

Pretend you are an archaeologist and you have discovered the artifacts of your life.

The articles that are around you right now, what do they say about you?

What can we tell about your priorities, how you spend your time, and what is important to you?

What conclusion would an archeologist make about you and your life?

FEBRUARY 5

Do you have any big dreams or vision that are living in the back of your mind?

Imagine that you are to indeed go after your dream.

What would it take?

What shift of your being would need to happen?

And what might one step be toward the vision? Take that one step today.

FEBRUARY 6

Models are taught to walk with their hips leading the way. This is because the hips are the strongest part of the body, and with the hips leading the way the rest of the body falls elegantly into place.

It is the same for us.

Leading from our strengths, ensures that the rest of who we are elegantly falls into place.

My strength is different from yours and yours is different from mine.

So, we make no comparisons. We simply get on with leading from our hips.

FEBRUARY 7

There is a whole segment of the population
that goes through life waiting on permission
and giving permission.

Yet permission is basically approval gone bad.

Taken to its farthest logical conclusion permission
makes and keeps us all as children.

Subscribing to permission based living gives way
too much authority to the thoughts and opinions
of others.

Bad idea. Advice and counsel, for sure.

Approval and permission, no way.

I don't know about you but for me it is time
to grow up a bit more.

FEBRUARY 8

Words are incredibly powerful.

They hold in them the power of cursing
or blessing. But of course only one or the
other at any given moment.

FEBRUARY 9

Taking a simple light and imposing a constraint upon it we end up with an exceptionally powerful tool called a laser.

For those in creative types of work where time is at our command and where options are endless, it is imperative to find and implement our own constraints.

Inviting and creating constraint around our time and work creates a catalyst resulting in fine-tuned and powerful results.

FEBRUARY 10

'Hi Rick, I am sorry I've taken so long to call you back. My life has been a little topsy-turvy as of late.'

Did you catch what is wrong here? An excuse has been made.

The first part is great for making a simple apology is always appropriate.

Making excuses on the other hand erodes our credibility.

No stories, no excuses, ever.

Thoughts

FEBRUARY 11

Gratitude grounds us in strength and resiliency.

When we can be thankful for the smallest things
even when they appear in the biggest messes,
we find a strength that no one can take away from us.

Practice the art of gratitude today, 'Thank-you for the
soft slippers on my feet, the warm cup of coffee in my
hand, and the soft light of the day.'

Settled by heart and mind into the smallest blessings
of our days garners profound strength.

Be strengthened today.

FEBRUARY 12

There are things that discourage us.

When we first encounter difficulties they tend
to stop us in our tracks.

Yet we soon learned this is counterproductive.
It was then we learned to push through difficulties
and to keep on keeping on.

With our muscles of tenacity and dogged
determination growing bit by bit.

One day after years of practice the time arrives
when all that comes against us actually serves to
propel us forward with greater focus and intensity.

A profound shift: when difficulties become a gift.

Thoughts

FEBRUARY 13

How might it change your life if you could clearly perceive that every single difficulty, every 'bad' thing even, has in fact been equipping you for the best things you bring to the world.

It appears that great works come out of the most difficult realities of our lives.

The gift of seeing this gives us strength to let go of bitterness and of that sense of being confounded and away from any need for retribution.

Rather, we take all that energy and put it into our own personal great work with stunning results.

FEBRUARY 14

'Enjoy life with the one you love,
Go, eat your bread with joy,
and drink your wine with a merry heart,
for God has already approved what you do.'

Ecclesiastes 9:7

FEBRUARY 15

Each one of us can find something we can
speak authoritatively about.

Each one of us has something that we are expert
in and able to bring to the table.

Speaking with authority comes from passion most
often born of struggle and difficulty. And because
we have done the hard work of pressing through,
learning more, testing and adjusting what we know
to what and how life really works, we bring
indispensable wisdom for others.

Bring your expertise that even one person
might be impacted.

FEBRUARY 16

We dream and we make plans, we set goals and establish our direction.

And then we hold it all with loose hands.

Open hands.

We pour our identity, our character, our habits, and our passions into the plans and goals.

But we always remember that we are not the sum total of these things.

We are so much more.

Thoughts

FEBRUARY 17

With every new season of life we have
fresh opportunity to revisit how we want
to be in the world.

What kind of person are we presenting?

What is the message we are giving?

Occasionally asking, 'How well is that working
for me?' and creating some shift.

Once we know how we want to be in this world,
there is not a single circumstance, easy or
difficult that can impede this.

We are solid.

FEBRUARY 18

Great figure skaters fully engage both the spins
and the set-up to the spins.

Before the great work of a spin, there is the
pause, the gathering of resources and inner
strength necessary for the spin.

So to in our lives.

Great works are preceded by a pause for the pause
is just as important as the great work. For here
is where the gathering of momentum and
clarity and vision is found.

When we are okay with the pauses of life,
we will be good to go with the great works.

FEBRUARY 19

What season is it for you?

Planting, growing, harvesting, perhaps
turning over a new plot of ground.

Whichever it is invest deeply in the
primary task at hand.

The hard work of digging ground, the
methodical care of planting, the patient nurture
of growing, or the thorough job of harvesting,
whichever it is for you right now, go after that
heart and soul with great focus and care and
you will be well equipped to succeed at each
season as it comes.

FEBRUARY 20

There is something vitally important about the timing of our lives. Have you noticed that given some time things that you were once trying to make happen fell into place when the timing was right.

Looking back it is easy to see this.

Going forward it is critical to remember this!

A great query, "How might I move in greater rhythm with the timing of my life?"

FEBRUARY 21

One of the key characteristics of courage
is audacity. Somewhere along the line we learned
that it was not a good thing to be audacious.

Perhaps something we need to relearn.

Where might you need a touch (or a lot) more audacity?

Audacity played out over the long haul . . .

Consider this: 'Where might I be, ten years
of audacity later?'

FEBRUARY 22

Alignment is all about lining up vision and passion and authority. It is the place where we have 'say' about and over life in general and specifically.

Actively and fully engaging the 'say' that uniquely belongs to each of us we find life starts to fall into place, it all starts to make sense and quite simply we find joy.

Keep your say, use it for yourself, and then invest it for others. It's how the world is changed, one 'say' at a time.

Thoughts

FEBRUARY 23

What is your great work?

A great work is what each of us uniquely brings
to the world by the power of our presence and being.

Great works are NOT what we are doing,
but about who we are.

Great works are elusive and hard to name.

Accustomed to seeing products and efforts
in a 'doing' kind of way, great works stem from
a much deeper place, and we must adjust our
vision to perceive them.

And while it may take years to name our great work,
we find that living our Great Work not only deeply
satisfies ourselves but everyone around us.

We are simply, a little more glad.

Thoughts

FEBRUARY 24

What are you NOT talking about?

Often the most important and close-to-our-heart passions and dreams are the very things we rarely mention.

Today, give yourself permission to mention in some small way that thing you have always thought of doing and the person you have always thought of being.

We'd really like to celebrate ALL of who you are!

FEBRUARY 25

It is absolutely critical to have clarity over our lives.

Clarity tunes and then fine-tunes our direction
and best efforts. Without clarity we are doing
a great job at something we aren't to be about
in the first place.

Not so effective.

Ask yourself, 'How would increased clarity improve
the quality of my days?'

What would you NOT be about?

Gaining clarity is never be a waste of time.
Get it at any cost. Your days depend on it!

Thoughts

FEBRUARY 26

Every goal, every task even, has multiple steps.

Feelings of overwhelm often result from taking
on these multiple steps all at once in the guise
of one goal or task.

Compassion for ourselves starts by giving
ourselves a bit of slack and is then worked
out by breaking those things we want to be
about into very small bits.

Accomplishing one small bit one thing at a time
sets us up for success. One small thing done today
another small thing tomorrow and so on, gets
us where we want to be.

Success breeding success

It's good for our hearts.

FEBRUARY 27

When we need something from someone
we have no ability for compassion.

And compassion drives development.

As long as we need others to be a certain way
for us, we in fact block development of that person.

Need demands.
Compassion meets.

FEBRUARY 28

We all have a natural way of dealing with difficulties. Some of us push hard against trouble and others of us back away.

Hard-wired and ingrained in us our preferred manner can be rounded out by other strategies.

We become adept at various responses to trouble. Unless there is stress. Stress takes us back to our natural default setting with increased vigor.

Those of us who naturally back away, will back away even further. And those of us who push hard towards, will push even harder. Not necessarily so bad except when difficulty, trouble, and stress is a person.

When backing farther away or pushing harder towards are never the best options.

FEBRUARY 29

A theory of access is simply knowing how to get
that raise, be accepted into that school, or become
a leader within an organization.

Every organization, every business, every social
group even, has a code of access. And it always boils
down to building rapport and establishing trust.

The quickest way to build rapport and establish trust,
is to study the leader/s. Find out who they are, what
their values are, how the organization works.

Matching yourself to the core goals and primary
values of an organization, you build deep rapport
which leads to significant trust and advancement.

March

TAKING ONE DAY AT A TIME

MARCH 1

We have run from limitation for so long that we don't understand it is a powerful tool.

Simply put: applying limitation to our work produces better work.

Whether the limitation is imposed on our time spent at a task, the number of words we prepare for a speech, or any number of ways we might apply this.

Bottom line: 'How might I utilize limitation to create my own powerful results?'

MARCH 2

When things go wrong we usually try to make
them right. It is human nature.

Yet, consider that what has gone wrong is simply
an opportunity for grand shifts and a great resettling
of energy and effort and focus.

What if the 'wrong' is simply granting time and
space to have it more 'right' than ever before.

To be sure, it is hard standing one foot on what
was, and one foot on what is to be.

Yet, wow! What opportunity there is for a remixing
of our lives into something we could have never
before imagined, if things had gone right.

MARCH 3

There is a whole group of folks that are tired
and burnt out. With everything resting on them
they have little time and don't want to take on
another thing.

Protection is the name of the game. Protection
of reputation, time, energy, resources . . . everything
is scarce, and people are a threat when you are in
protection mode.

But there is another group of people who operate
on the power of who they are and not what they are
doing. Where they experience enough of everything
because they are working in synergy and collaboration
with many other folk.

These ones know that people are our only true
resource, and that we are rich beyond measure
when we take the risk to deeply work alongside
others. In company of others we take on more
and find we are doing less.

MARCH 4

Our most valuable resource are the people around us. Learning this takes some risk. It takes some transparency. It takes some courage.

It takes humility.

The wealthy know that in order to succeed we do so on the recommendations, the connections, the endorsements, and the help of those who can open doors for us.

The wealthy understand people as wealth. Which interesting to note, turns into a wealth of resources.

MARCH 5

In the world of rules and the 'way things should be' we get a little stuck on what is right and wrong.

Right and wrong often simply boiling down to a lot of man-made structure to control and manipulate the world around us.

Personal development to be solid and true must move from right and wrong (the place of a child either submitting to or reacting against) to what works.

Maturity looks at what works (and what doesn't work) and makes decisions from there.

Thoughts

TAKING ONE DAY AT A TIME

MARCH 6

The American Music Awards are a grand example of artists come together to honour one another: to celebrate and award each other's successes.

Quite simply one of the reasons why success follows on success for these folks.

For when we honour others, we ourselves will find honour.

Celebrating others paves a road for personal celebration. You get the picture.

Success follows those who applaud other's successes. Honouring, celebrating, applauding are always the very best of investments.

MARCH 7

Each of us have the power to hold and to
create any kinds of spaces simply by the essence
of who we are.

By our intentions, by our focus on life, our attitude,
and the lenses through which we perceive, we hold
spaces of either criticism or empathy, antagonism
or welcome, disdain or respect, and so on.

It is therefore critical to understand, to accept
and to take responsibility for the kinds of spaces
we hold for others, and then to simply ask ourselves,
'What kinds of spaces do I want to be holding?'

MARCH 8

Coaches understand that dissatisfaction is the starting point of all change.

In fact: Dissatisfaction X Vision X First Steps > Resistance to Change

We do not stay in dissatisfaction for long but we use it to propel us to a vision of what we do want.

We then gain clarity of what our first steps are toward that vision: all of which adds up to something greater than our resistance to change.

We need all three parts for change to happen: Dissatisfaction, Vision, and First Steps

Leave any of those out and we only get what we've always ever got.

MARCH 9

Evidence reveals that the more successful
the person the longer the time-frame that person
is working from.

Living for today or this week is never a winning model.

Our vision must go further and beyond ourselves
to truly become something of impact.

Those who think and work with time frames of ten,
twenty, even fifty years, make key decisions differently
than those who can only see to the end of next year.
Stretch out your thinking in terms of time and see
what changes for you.

MARCH 10

100% responsibility is an extremely powerful
place from which to live our lives.

Taking 100% responsibility for where and how
our lives are at this very moment results in profound
shifts in the way we do life.

Assuming 100% responsibility doesn't mean that
everything is due to you, it is simply an extremely
powerful space and way to come into our realities.

What might change if you were to assume
100% responsibility?

MARCH 11

Convictions:
We either have our own or we live another's.

We are either established in our own or in insecurity
we impose them on others.

We either stand in the strength of our own convictions
or we stand in the way of others convictions.

Creating truly powerful collaborations only happens
once the hard work of differentiation is complete.

That powerful place where each of us stand solid
in our conviction, neither taking on others as our own,
and neither expecting others to live ours.

MARCH 12

A conviction is simply a call to action.

For us.

The mistake we make is to confuse our conviction
as a call to action for someone else.

Simply, if you feel strongly about something
put some legs to it yourself.

Holding back, expecting and waiting for others
to take on your call to action, is most often
a losing proposition.

Whether the conviction is best described
as a calling or a dream or a vision doesn't matter,
however you call it, it is calling you to action.

MARCH 13

On the way to profound collaborations we must
first find our own success as it relates to time.
The following questions are simply opportunity
to take a bit of time: gaining further clarity:

'Where am I spending too much time?'

'Where am I spending too little time?'

'What do I do that could be eliminated?'

'What do I do that could be delegated or shared?'

Thoughts

MARCH 14

Gaining clarity is the hardest work we will ever do.

We would much rather grunt through tasks,
put in a good days work, even tackle a difficult
conversation than gain clarity.

To gain clarity we must be willing to consider
that some (or a lot) of how and why we are doing
life may not be accurate. This requires putting
ourselves on the line in and we can't control what'll
stick and what won't.

Without clarity we may be doing an amazing job
at something we aren't even supposed to be about,
the ultimate waste.

Bottom line: Clarity requires focus and energy, time
and risk.

Not for the faint of heart.

Thoughts

MARCH 15

We are often hardest on ourselves.

When we are hard on ourselves we become
hard on others, as we can only give out what
we ourselves have.

For instance if we do not know grace we cannot
give grace. If we do not know the benefit of the doubt
extended we cannot give benefit of the doubt.

Therefore the best gift we give ourselves
and ultimately to others is the gift of
compassionate inquiry.

When you deal with yourself do so with compassion.

Thoughts

TAKING ONE DAY / AT A TIME

MARCH 16

The true leader is the one who is most emotionally mature. This is because our limbic system, the seat of emotion within our beings, is an open system.

Our nervous system, respiratory system, and other systems are closed systems. Your blood pressure is not affected by another's blood pressure for instance. Whereas we are affected by others emotions.

Group (ie: family, work, organizational, church, etc.) members will automatically and intuitively orient to the one who is most emotionally aware.

Quite simply, this is why if you want to lead and create influence you must do hard emotional work.

Only this earns you the right to have others pay attention to you and to follow your lead.

MARCH 17

We will not see miracles happen in our own
lives or the lives of others unless we are willing
to do hard emotional labour.

Miracles quite simply (and by whatever definition you use)
are driven by love, that hardest emotional work of all.

Love is full engagement (that does not back away)
of another person's reality no matter how painful
or atrocious or devastating.

This empathy then drives vision and the ability to see
the person beyond their present state.

Vision drives declaration ('this will not be!') and declaration
drives action. Action that changes the fabric and landscape
of a person's life.

Waiting for a miracle will never bring a miracle, for we are
the ones who either engage them or not.

MARCH 18

What do you want?

Connecting with our passion is some of the
hardest work we will ever do. Knowing what we want
and then risking to say it is very important work.

Intuitively knowing what we want, the trick
is being willing to connect with it, own it and
make the changes necessary to cooperate
with it, all of which equals huge risk.

What do you want?

A question that separates the passive from
the engaged and the followers from the leaders.

What do you want?

MARCH 19

Fully connecting with our passion is scary business.
In the midst of being fully engaged we may say and
do things that we later wonder, "What was I thinking?!"

While far too easy to doubt ourselves we can
rest (or shake) in the knowledge that the fruit
of our full engagement is determined by where
we draw our strength.

If our strength comes from negativism and criticism
and suspicion and the likes, then our fruit will be
riddled with the same.

If our strengths flow from the affirmative, the positive,
the welcoming, and the likes, then our fruit will be
full of the same.

A life is made by the strengths we take on
and passionate engagements tell no lies.

MARCH 20

A coaching friend declares: no matter what the circumstance or difficulty try asking this, 'How is this the best thing that ever happened to me?'

Try it right now. Practice, really take it on, and feel your mind opening to new possibilities and opportunities.

What did you think? How does that feel?

What might change for you in light of that question?

A simple question that if you let it will make all the difference in the world.

MARCH 21

Our irritations reveal the heart of our matters.

Jealousy with those who have achieved something
that we are shrinking from or waiting for, is common.

In the face of a success that we ourselves are
wired for but not yet ready to own, jealousy is the
only logical response of the heart. Yet before we
can admit jealousy we simply find irritation.

Walls of irritation and jealousy may keep us from
the vulnerability of naming our destiny, may keep us
disconnected from our own desires and gifted places,
but they will never satisfy the deepest longings of our
lives. We will merely end up with wasted years.
What or who is irritating you?

Let this tell you something.

MARCH 22

Wanting to increase our intellectual knowledge
we glean from those smarter than us.

We read books, listen to lectures, take classes.
Wanting to increase our emotional repertoire
we also glean from those smarter than us.

We watch movies, listen to music, take in music
videos, go to art galleries and plays and read
some poetry.

Depending on whether you lead from an intellectual
strength or an emotional strength, the one is fairly
easy the other is not.

Neither one is more right or wrong than the other.

Both are absolutely necessary.

MARCH 23

Know who your enemies are.

Just as important as gathering a team around you is the discernment to know who is NOT for you.

Not everyone has your best interest at heart.

Do you know who they are?

MARCH 24

About only 15% of communication are the words we speak.

The remaining 85% of communication is body language, tone, facial expressions, and emotions.

It is why, if we are listening with our hearts we don't always have to get the words or understand the language.

Listening with our hearts we are well equipped for:

- meeting others at the heart of matters
- serving them in this place
- creating collaborations based on these meetings
- forging strategic alliances going forward

Listening with heart: a mark of the best leaders.

MARCH 25

Leading in generosity errs us on
the side of good will.

Giving others the benefit of the doubt
removes from us suspicious living.

Both parties win.

MARCH 26

Classic coaching questions:

What do you want?

How might you get it?

How might you deepen your commitment to it?

How will you know when you've got it?

MARCH 27

Moving forward always has us bumping up against fear. Once dormant, fear in the face of new challenges would have us back down, give up, and stand aside from opportunity.

But fear fed this way merely increases.

Rather, when we admit our fear, 'I am afraid' we are then free to get on with the work at hand, both the opportunities and the challenges.

Energy is released towards expansion instead of staying safe.

A worthwhile trade.

Thoughts

TAKING ONE DAY / AT A TIME

MARCH 28

Priorities are not just about the things we are doing, but about the spaces we leave in our lives.

What kind of margin do you want to establish?

All sorts of things come up unexpected. How are you planning for them?

What potential opportunities are you deliberately establishing space and margin that you might move nimbly and quickly at the right time?

Priorities must not only go to the immediate here and now, but even more so, to what might be.

Thoughts

MARCH 29

Taking the time to let go of and to grieve things
of our lives, makes way for what can be new.

It isn't easy. Grief never is.

But acknowledging, thanking, and releasing what
is no longer necessary or needed or healthy even
simply and profoundly, makes way.

Thoughts

MARCH 30

It is critical to separate ourselves from
our judgments about things. We can often see
this and that and correctly so. The difficulty
is when we are attached to the observation.

At these times we layer what we see with meaning,
and that is where we get into trouble.

The meaning we add is often the incorrect part
and the part we own and thus the part that connects
us to the judgment.

To see and judge correctly we must refrain
from adding meaning (let the meaning show
up for itself).

Thoughts

TAKING ONE DAY AT A TIME

MARCH 31

If you are feeling in over your head,
you are in exactly the right spot.

Going after more than what logically makes
sense is opportunity bar none.

There is no other way to become something
bigger than ourselves than to lose the security
of playing safe within ourselves.

April

TAKING ONE / DAY AT A TIME

APRIL 1

Hold spaces of honour.

For men, for women, for children, for the elderly.

Make room in your life to invest and care
and pour into others.

And you will find deep honour
coming back your way.

Honour and you will be honoured.

APRIL 2

Heart, will, and risk are the three key ingredients to any idea coming into reality.

All three must be present.

Heart: the passion to go after something.
Will: the grit to put legs and effort to the work.
Risk: the ultimate test of both heart and will; what are you willing to put on the line to ensure success?

Have any two and not the third and your ideas will fade into dust.

Which one do you need a touch more of today?

Thoughts

APRIL 3

The heart of coaching:

What is the outcome you want?

When do you want it?

How will you know you are successful?

When you are successful what else will improve?

What resources are available to you?

How can I support you?

What are you going to do now to get what you want?

APRIL 4

Mindsets of sufficiency or conversely mindsets
of scarcity have nothing to do with our circumstances
or surroundings.

Scarcity thinking can be found in the most
lush of circumstances.

And sufficiency is found in the poorest of surroundings.

We decide whether we come from a place
of scarcity or sufficiency.

Which will it be for you?

APRIL 5

There are many times in life when we have
no clue what comes next.

This not-knowing can stop us short.

We freeze.

The trick is to just start in, get going, move forward
with what little might be present, and the rest
begins to fall in place.

APRIL 6

Solutions are always right at hand,
even if we can't see them.

Think of your most pressing situation.

What might the solution be hiding behind?

Thoughts

APRIL 7

Regardless of the trials and set-backs that
seem to take the wind out of our sails, constancy
of person shines through.

It is the element of comfort and sameness that
even when everything seems up in the air little
things are still the same.

Increasing our own constancy, and the comfort
and sameness that we can offer to others comes
down to simply settling into our own skin just
that much more.

Living the sameness of you creates constancy
for those around you.

Thank-you for that.

APRIL 8

We can live primarily from either
our minds or our hearts.

The first gets the job done.

The second turns the job into an art form.

APRIL 9

It is most important to pay attention
to the rhythms and seasons of our lives.

The fallow times build up strength
for the growing times.

The fruit-bearing seasons lay a harvest
for the lean times.

Each kind of season and rhythm
is absolutely necessary.

APRIL 10

Successful people get help.

They take and give referrals and recommendations.

They hire office and book-keeping
assistance as needed.

They have financial advisers, legal representation,
medical specialists and spiritual elders.

They outsource tasks that are not natural strengths.

They build support around themselves in virtually
every area of their lives.

They hire coaches, counsellors, prayer ministers,
With physical trainers, physiotherapists, chiropractor
and massage

Taking care of body and soul and life
requires support.

Successful people know they
cannot succeed without others.

APRIL 11

Moving along the path towards
mastery finds us letting go of many things.

We quite often start off with multiple
and numerous things we like to do, are good
at doing, and feel compelled to do.

Mastery demands that we let much
(dare I say most) of this go.

The path narrows the closer we are to our
core passion and expression.

Letting go of things we like and are good at
and compelled to do, is hard.

Mastery has us doing less yet with greater
impact. We simply do not have to pad our lives
with the superfluous.

APRIL 12

How many of us back off from
projects because of overwhelm?

We resonate with a large task or a profound vision
or a passionate response to something. We feel
the call to engage in something bigger than ourselves.
Yet we like being the center of the picture, and we are
pretty committed to self-preservation.

Feelings of inadequacy are merely symptoms
of us still in the picture. Fear of being too proud
or self-important is the same thing.

Either response: it is still all about us.

It's why we shrink from vision and passion.
We intuitively know that our concerns, our fears,
our pride, will have to stand at the sidelines.

And pride does not easily stand aside.

Thoughts

APRIL 13

Friendly or familiar.

Many social and business mistakes are made
when we are familiar with people too soon.

Friendly draws others in. Friendly develops rapport
and a sense of safety with a person.

But familiar this must be reserved and saved for later.

Only when the other person signals that familiar
is okay, do we act in a familiar way.

APRIL 14

Freedom is choice between two viable options.

If either option has not been fully faced then choice boils down to personal default settings which is not freedom.

Facing all possibilities internally, while emotionally and psychologically working things through to logical conclusions, frees us to face 'either way'.

This is a strength of freedom and choice that can never be lost or taken away because it comes from deep inside us.

APRIL 15

When the pressure eases, when we catch up
with our work, when we are handed a touch
of unexpected time, maybe even an entire free
day, what do we do with it?

Do we accept and bask in the bounty: giving
ourselves some slack, or fret and worry about
the pressures of tomorrow?

One response recharges our lives, the other . . .

APRIL 16

In business we under-promise and over-deliver.

Rather than make a big ta-da about what
is to come up front we make modest claims
so we can quietly go about surpassing them.

It is smart to do the same in relationships.

Make no vows simply let your yes be yes
and your no be no.

Thoughts

APRIL 17

Physically speaking flexibility is the indicator
of strength. We can think of our emotional and
psychological in the same way.

The greater our flexibility the greater our strength.

It's why it is important to harness our breadth
of difficulties, making good use of them to expand
our responses to life.

We do have choice We can either become
more pinched and narrow when life strikes us hard
or we can push into the pain and let it expand our
internal resilience.

Pushed hard to flexibility both muscle and soul
respond marvellously if we let them.

Thoughts

APRIL 18

It appears that we do not easily
cooperate with the vision of our lives.

Perhaps it has never occurred to us that we
must agree with and participate with passion
and vision and our futures.

Perhaps we think that life comes to us,
that we can passively wait and all will fall into place.

It is like life gives us a hint of things to come
and then waits to see if we will agree or disagree.

Almost like life takes its cues from us.

APRIL 19

We may not know it but we are rich in knowledge.

Educated to the brim.

Taking our knowledge for granted we can fall prey
to believing we need more and then a bit more
as well in order to go forward.

And for sure sometimes this is true.

But what if the education and the knowledge you
have today is just right for the forward movement
you might want to take this year?

Thoughts

APRIL 20

Sameness, certainty and constancy wrap
us in comfort and security.

And while this comes to us from outside ourselves
through our environments and circumstances, real
strength and resilience begins when we carry these
things inside ourselves.

When we become constant, when we are certain
of who we are and our place in the world, and when
sameness flows from how we experience the world
and not in how the world comes to us, true strength
of self holds a firm place in the sand.

Once we have routine within our own beings
we take that wherever we may go and into whatever
environments that might challenge our security.

Comfort from the inside out.

APRIL 21

Some engage unless told to hold
back, others hold back unless told to engage.

Some give unless there is some good reason
not to, others will not give unless there is some
good reason to do so.

Some help as a matter of course, others
help only when convinced.

Paradigms are very strong filters through which
we make decisions, determine course, and gauge
day-to-day activities

If you find yourself confused when the opportunity
to engage, to give, or to help presents itself, you
just may need to change . . .

Instead of asking, "Should I?"
Ask, "Why not?"

APRIL 22

When things feel overwhelming and we find
ourselves irritated and nit-picking, it is crucial
to pull the camera lens back.

For sure there are times to zoom in on an aspect
of our life. In fact this is when critiques and
realignments and critical adjustments are made.

But we can't live long in this zoomed-in focus.
To maintain healthy perspective we must zoom out.

Seeing the big picture and the vision from the
sky is our saving in the face of being overwhelmed.

Everything simply takes on perspective while
overwhelmed, irritated and nit-picked tend to fall away.

APRIL 23

We can see the logic and wisdom of any given
course of action or decision by imagining it taken
to its farthest possible degree.

'If I carry this line of thinking to its farthest logical
conclusion, where am I?'

And if it is somewhere we don't want to be, something
we don't believe in, a way of being that is not of value
to us, then we must come back to adjust our thinking
and examine our paradigms.

Wisdom is only wisdom if it can be taken to its farthest
extreme and still works.

Wisdom, truth, purity, will only ever get more beautiful,
more pure, and more true.

Whereas false wisdom, tainted truth, and unjust
purity simply gets uglier and uglier and more damaging
the farther it is taken.

APRIL 24

The work of our lives is often obscured by life.

You know: the deadlines, the nitty-gritty,
the one-more-thing that is on our to-do list.

What saves us from this vortex that threatens
to take us down is the perspective of others over
our lives. We desperately need others as witness
of our lives.

Others that can say, "This is what I saw, and this
is what I see now."

We are immeasurably strengthened when we allow
others the privilege and opportunity to witness and
to speak into our lives.

Thoughts

APRIL 25

Waiting is hard work.

It tests our resolve,
our commitments and our character.

Nothing refines us as much as waiting.

Waiting also asks the question:

"What am I going to contribute to the conclusion?"

"How much do I really want this?"

Waiting brings forth passion and determined effort.

Well worth the wait.

April 26

Meditation, devotions, worship and thanksgiving, ground us to strength and resilience.

While these responses may initially begin as the responses of weak people in the face of great need, the habits of these create strong people; centering ourselves is never a waste of time.

Answers to hard questions, clarity over confusion and peace in the midst of upheaval are simply some of the gifts that come out of 'taking time aside'.

Going from strength to strength, that is our legacy.

APRIL 27

Be the wall.

One of the key's to raising healthy children
is to 'be the wall' often and early on in their lives.

Those who never had the benefit of parents 'being
the wall' never develop the character necessary to
positively respond to life.

They only ever know crushing 'woe is me' responses.
Disappointments must be reckoned well or we waste
copious amounts of energy trying to make perceived
offenses right.

Character Development 101: What is the 'wall' in your
life right now, and how are you responding?

APRIL 28

Markers tell us about our days.

They mark seasons and times
and the change of one stage into another.

It does not work very well to see the markers
when in the midst of them but looking back
creates an interesting picture.

If you were to write down 12 markers of your
own life (much like we mark the key paragraphs
in a book), what might they be?

Thoughts

APRIL 29

Compassion is the leverage
that takes all our efforts to that next level.

Compassion is the place where miracles happen,
where influence is for the person and not just for the
work and where hearts find companionship.

Because after all we are simply all the same and
with the same struggles and the same longings.

Compassion sees people as they truly
are and serves them there.

Compassion just might be the most powerful
force in the world.

APRIL 30

We are all better for finding those who help us speak
what we cannot quite find the words for ourselves.

Whether it be a favorite blog, music that touches
deep within, the local art gallery, or any number
of things, we are healthier inside and out when
we find our voice.

Mentors do this and are needed in all parts of life.

And while there are often mentors close by
and actively engaged in the mix of our lives
don't discount the subtle and indirect mentors.

Whether a singer, author, or artist, give them
space and time, welcome them in.

May

TAKING ONE DAY AT A TIME

MAY 1

Initiative moves forward.

Initiative doesn't get caught playing the victim.
It is too busy getting on with things.

Initiative makes no excuses.

Initiative gives no power away.
It holds the locus of control close to itself.

Knowing that waiting for others to make
something right rarely works.

Rather, initiative becomes
its own force to be reckoned with.

MAY 2

Everything we need to know
is completely open and available to us.

Applying that information is another matter.

While finding information is not difficult,
application is an entirely different matter.

Application is entirely up to us and is not easy.

And yet, application is what separates the common
from the not-so-common. Strategically, deliberately,
step by step application, making a plan and then
working the plan, sets leaders apart from followers
and the indispensable from the cogs in the wheels.

After all: Application trumps information.

MAY 3

Together anything can be accomplished,
Alone, some stuff can happen.

Together everything comes together,
Alone, we begin running out of options.

Together the simplest thing is leveraged
up and beyond,

Alone, everything comes to an end.

Making space for together, inviting it,
nurturing it, celebrating it . . .

What might we accomplish together?

MAY 4

Declaring our intentions is powerful.

Taking what is in our hearts and minds, forming words to these things, saying it out loud, creates movement all around us.

Nothing can stay the same once we have declared.

MAY 5

We seek after freedom never fully understanding
that it is found through responsibility.

The more responsibility we exhibit,
the more faithful we are.

The more we say, 'the buck stops here
and I refuse to make excuses', the more freedom.

Simple as that.

MAY 6

Others will offend us,
hurt us and we will experience disappointment.

What do we do?

We keep short accounts:

1. Name the offense (how are we hurt or offended?)

2. Remove attack and blame from the issue
   (settle into the hurt, allow it to wash over you)

3. Grieve (admit the disappointment)

4. State it how it is (I am hurt, disappointed
   and that offended me)

Not needing anything from the other person we've
validated our own process, given voice to the situation,
grieved the loss, and stated our truth, we are now
free to move forward.

MAY 7

Creativity and the most enjoyable kinds of productivity happen in this space we call the 'flow'; where we are centered, where ideas tumble out upon each other, and where possibility opens up.

It's the place where things happen.

The most important thing to know about flow is what sets the stage for you to enter into that flow state.

What are your requirements of surroundings, of rhythm, of rest, and any myriad of things.

How might you set the stage to enter your own flow-state more?

MAY 8

Advancement doesn't happen without faithfulness.

Faithfulness to the nitty-gritty and the mundane paves the way for the extraordinary and the grand.

What grand thing might you be heading for?

And what nitty-gritty and mundane needs attention to get you there?

Thoughts

MAY 9

The observations of those around us are invaluable
We cannot see or know everything there is to know
about ourselves.

Feedback from others is critical.

It is the super-power of anyone looking
for sustainable influence.

MAY 10

What makes you stand out from the crowd?

What are you bringing to the table
that others cannot do without?

What unique effect do you have upon people?

It doesn't have to be large or outrageous.

In fact the most significant influences
are often quite subtle.

One of a kind, you've got it, now build on it.

Thoughts

TAKING ONE DAY AT A TIME

MAY 11

New things and times and seasons
require that we leave the old behind.

Not without some grief and sorrow to be sure.
For space and energy and focus must all shift
from time to time.

And it isn't always nice by any means,
But it is always good.

MAY 12

Rest,
Change of pace,

An opportunity to do something out of the ordinary,
All gives refreshment.

And whether your rest day is Sunday or another day,
What might you do to shake things up a bit?

To use muscles different than the ordinary.

To see in a way not normally seen.

To perceive with a wider lens.

Thoughts

MAY 13

The best time to work: When is that for you?

Some love the mornings,
others mid-afternoon, or even the night.

It doesn't matter when but it is important to
know your best time to get things done and to
protect that time fiercely.

Don't do the dishes or laundry during that time.

Don't wash the car or fix that shelf during that time.

Ask yourself, "What specific things need doing to
advance my career and business and life?"

Then do ONLY these things during your best time.

MAY 14

The art of perception must be
honed separately from the art of meaning.

To perceive is to observe.

Adding the meaning to our observations,
to do it well, requires an absence of our ego.

Not many of us are able to perceive without
adding our ego into the mix.

But those who can perceive without ego,
they are the wise and most beneficial amongst us.

Hone your perception, and leave your ego out of it.

MAY 15

How do you process overwhelm?

Overwhelm comes in that shifting place
between big picture clarity and small focus results.

We are either taking in our lives and work as though
standing far off, or we are taking in our lives and work
close up and in detail.

Both are required, yet it is that place between
the two where overwhelm can strike.

Don't let yourself hang in that never-never land.
At any given moment determine whether your immediate
focus is on the big picture or on the small details and
take action accordingly.

MAY 16

What would a time-lapse
camera reveal about your days?

Take yesterday for instance.
Imagine: see in your mind's eye your entire
day as through a time-lapse camera

What would it show?

What might you discover?

And how might that impact your days to come?

MAY 17

Encouraging, applauding, validating,
simple work that we can do every single day.

Work that leaves profound impact,

Work that moves hearts and lives,

Work that takes but moments.

Feedback in terms of specific observations
and affirmations empowers our lives beyond
what we could ever imagine.

Today, simply affirm another,
and then another, and another.

MAY 18

Replacing ourselves is a must.

Unless there is someone trained and ready
to take over our position we will never be able
to step into that next phase or place.

Who trains our replacements?

We do.

We are the ones most invested in our own
life. Therefore we take the responsibility
of our forward motion.

What might you do to invest in those coming
up behind you and how might you prepare your
own steps forward?

MAY 19

There is a distinct reality to the timing
of things in our lives.

Experienced intuitively and often at those
peripheral glances, timing is to be respected
and worked with, not against.

Timing is just that: Timing

If it is off, whole projects end up being 'off'.
If it is on, everything gains momentum and spins
into a life of its own.

Honor timing and time will honor you.

Thoughts

MAY 20

When things don't go 'right' what do we do?

Perhaps we forget that we are perfectly wired
for even the things that don't go well.

Perhaps we have all we need for crisis and upset.

Perhaps and in fact, if we draw deep enough from
within our internal reserves, we will find a genius
for dealing with difficulty that we never knew we
had and never would have known we had . . .

Except that the 'not right' showed up to reveal it.

MAY 21

When tempted to live outside of today, when
concern or worry about tomorrow or the next week
begin to pile up, gratitude brings us back to today.

And not the 'I am so glad to have a home' kind
of gratitude, something even more specific than this.
A kind of gratitude that grounds us into this very
moment wherever you are.

Like this: "It is early, the sun is beginning to rise,
I am thankful for windows that I might see out, and
for the couch where I am sitting. The fireplace is on,
tea is being prepared, my housecoat is warm
and I am glad for this moment."

Gratitude that affirms our very moment, bringing
us back to right now, is exactly what we need when
tomorrow or the next week encroaches on today.

MAY 22

Questions are incredibly valuable.
They are in fact often more valuable than answers.

Questions open up our mind and our options,
While answers often dictate a conclusion,

Sometimes before any conclusion should be made.

Holding questions as though in the palm of our
open hand, allowing inquiry and investigation of
sorts is certainly a learned skill.

What part of your life might benefit
from a period of inquiry?

MAY 23

Everything about us is muscle.
The ability to work is a muscle.

To love is a muscle.

Menial tasks, routines, relationships, rest, play,
communication, community, and more, all muscle.

Muscles grow through difficulty.

Muscles become strong through resistance.

'Adversity doesn't happen to you, it happens for you.'

MAY 24

Rest is hard to find
in the midst of too many possessions.

Things pile up, space runs out.
In North America we have death by stuff.

How might you pare down your world?

And if you were to take three boxes to
goodwill this week, would you really miss
anything? Would your life be less-than in
any way?

And what might be the gains?

MAY 25

Honor is at the core of all success.
Where we give out honor we will receive honor.

What honor are you missing in your life?

And whom might you honor today?

MAY 26

Simple appreciation proves anything but simple.

"I think you are great" goes farther than
one can ever imagine.

"Boy I like you" can make someone's day.

Appreciation is in the repertoire of any great person.

Sticking with us forever appreciation need not be
extravagant, only accurate, sincere and simple.

MAY 27

Sincerity wins the day any day.

Balderdash, jesting, teasing, are all like potato chips: junk food that should be eaten sparingly.

Sincerity on the other hand has a place at every meal and in every conversation and throughout every day.

Sincerity is substance that nourishes.

Thoughts

MAY 28

What makes you glad?

What brings a spring to your step?

What leaves you smiling ear to ear?

What wraps joy around you?

Do that today.

MAY 29

There is a timing to things that cannot be swayed.

Effort poured in before the 'fullness' of time feels
like wasted effort; before its 'time' we cannot make
something come to be despite our very best efforts.

And then once the 'time' has arrived nothing can
stop it. Much like a babe in the womb and then born,
the waiting and waiting seems to go on forever.

But once that babe's time has come, nothing
can stop it, all of creation conspires to bring
that child into the world.

Our part: we simply prepare, and invest,
and wait and trust, and be at the ready,

It'll happen.

MAY 30

A good meal is to be savored with all of one's senses brought to bear upon the experience.

Pausing all action and planning and execution of ideas simply enhances and makes great the tastes and textures. We don't miss anything

So too is life.

What part of life might taste better if savored?

MAY 31

By what standard do we gauge 'right'? And by what standard are things all of a sudden 'wrong'?

There certainly are things that do indeed go wrong, often very wrong. But what about those things that feel wrong simply because they are not what we are used to,

or expect,

or count on,

or want?

Maybe it's our standard that needs to shift.

TAKING ONE *June* DAY AT A TIME

JUNE 1

Pressure increases the closer we get to that goal.

Pressure tests our resolve.

Pressure ensures our character can carry the work.

If we can withstand pressure we can withstand
all that comes with goals realized.

New levels of consistency, stability, dependability,
requires just a bit of pressure to get there.

JUNE 2

Formulation is the first step on our way to Mastery. It's the place of declaration about whom and what we are and how we want to be in the world.

Formulations operate out of language and create gigantic shifts in our beings, deep within.

Once we've formulated, once we've declared nothing quite looks the same ever again.

Once we've declared, we are changed, and the world must change with us.

JUNE 3

Six of the most powerful words in the English language:

"How can I help you today?"

Try asking someone this today,
And prepare to have your socks blown
off when someone asks you.

Powerful words. Give them a try.

JUNE 4

Being the best you can be
means you are setting the standard.

You are the benchmark
by which others gauge themselves.

It starts by setting your own standards,
holding firm to your own benchmarks.

Firming up your own standards simply yet
profoundly moves you toward the best you
can be and others will sit up, take notice,
and draw from your example.

JUNE 5

As a kid we were good at . . .

As a teenager we were good at . . .

At twenty we were good at . . .

At thirty we were good at . . .

Notice that what we were good at during our
childhood, moved us into what we were good
at in our teens.

What we were good at in our teens moved
us into our twenties . . .

What you are good at today is not yet the end
of the road. It is meant to move you into something
more. Sometimes it is simply about taking the risk
to let go of our 'good at today' so that the 'good
at tomorrow' can take its place.

JUNE 6

In service to others means it is not about us.

Somewhere along the line we must know ourselves
and own ourselves well enough to begin pouring us
out, risking to lose ourselves in something bigger
than ourselves.

Knowing that as we pour out we are poured into.
Always risking to give it all away we find we have
more than before.

JUNE 7

After a particularly confusing day or week
a time of silence is necessary.

Trust that a few days of introspection won't
ruin a thing. Take time to stand back and take
in all parameters.

Allow the peripheral voices to fall away.
Resulting in better decisions, and more
clarity going forward,

Something none of us can afford to do without.

JUNE 8

Having said it before, it's worth saying again:

Taking 100% percent responsibility,
Carrying the full weight of a problem,
Shifts us from average,

To extraordinary.

Take 100% responsibility regularly and routinely,
And you will stand heads above the crowd.

Thoughts

JUNE 9

Consistency counts.

Not in big grandiose ways, rather it is the small things, the little details that make the most impact and establish us as trustworthy or not.

If you might shift one little detail today, towards greater professionalism, what might that be?

And what is the long-range cost if you don't?

JUNE 10

Keeping our cool in a meeting,
Requires we:

    1. Know where we stand on the issue

    2. Know where we can compromise

    3. And where we cannot compromise

Negotiations need not be too messy.
They simply need a bit of grace, a lot of guts,
and a good dose of clarity.

JUNE 11

Tracking the numbers allows for increase.

Whether its money in the bank, hits on a website, or time to accomplish a task, tracking tells us at a glance where we've been, where we are, and where we are going.

Regardless of how bad the numbers are when we begin, starting allows for that incremental growth to be noticed and celebrated.

Our confidence grows, our number savvy puts down deeper roots, we are better established, and ready for the increase.

JUNE 12

Repetition is one way to
learn something and have it stick.

Whatever we are taking in we must
'practice it out'. For then we know it.

They say it takes ten-thousand hours to reach
Mastery; that place where what we know comes
intuitively flowing out of who we are.

Make sure you are putting your time
where you want Mastery to be the result.

Make sure your practice hours and your repetition
is an investment in the big picture and the final goal.

You don't want to be Master of just anything.

JUNE 13

Know your parameters.

Structure around the outside
of your work creates efficiency and focus,

Efficiency and focus create powerful results.
High ceilings in a work space make room for
creativity, Low ceilings establish space for
planning and decision making.

It's similar with everything we do,
Pay attention to the lay-out, the parameters,
be them on the page, in a room or through the
rhythm of your day,

Parameters affect us. Know how they affect
you and use them to create powerful results.

JUNE 14

What makes you angry?

What fires up your passion, igniting a fire in your belly? That thing,

Go do something about it.

JUNE 15

Ready or not, the time for action arrives.

We cannot go our whole lives preparing
for the work. At some point in time the
work must take place.

Once that time has been reached every
single thing we have learned or not learned,
will be revealed in the mix.

So the question must be asked:
Are we soaking in the lessons of today?

JUNE 16

Opposition comes. No doubt about that.

Question being: how do we navigate it?

Ease and peace and comfort
will never test us the way that difficulty does.

Difficulty grows our internal muscles like nothing else.

One day we'll even be thankful for it, every last bit.

Thoughts

JUNE 17

Are we dependent on things going well?

What if things don't go well? Would that
really affect who we are and what we are about?

Are we basing our actions and peace on
circumstances or on a solid core of values
and vision?

Hint: Go for the latter.

JUNE 18

What was once so hard is now easy,
What was once unimaginable, becomes common-place.

Therefore, the difficulty today,
Will become your place of ease tomorrow.

It is the way of learning and of life,
Of forward movement and maturity.

Take heart.

JUNE 19

Of all the good things you
can do, what might you really be about?

If you had to prioritize your interests,
which ones would come out first, second and third.

If you could do only one, which might it be?

JUNE 20

Sensitivity is often scoffed, looked down upon
as weak and spineless, and a vulnerable position
to be 'fixed'.

But is this really true?

Perhaps sensitivity is the hallmark of an artist,

Perhaps it is the first sign of a master,
One who feels deeply,
Thinks deeply,
Who listens intently, and ministers profoundly.

But for a few more sensitive folk in our midst.

JUNE 21

Some things we are asked to do poorly.

The only way to begin is often to struggle
and not have it up to par.

And while these scenarios test our resolve
and humility,

We often learn the most from mistakes.

If we must have success ensured before we begin,
There is not much we would begin.

Everything has a lesson in it, growth to be had from it,
If we don't mind doing it poorly at the start.

Thoughts

JUNE 22

Decisions:

Some are anxious until a decision is made, others become anxious once a decision is made.

Which are you?

Do you drive towards decisions, or stay far back from them? This one characteristic will explain a lot of how you do life.

JUNE 23

A lot of people have the HEART for something.

"Yes that would be great"

"Wow that would be amazing"

But fewer people have the WILL: Where actions
and muscle and discipline must be applied to what
the heart wants.

And even less have the RISK: Where one enters
and engages an idea lock-stock-and-barrel and
where idea becomes reality.

Nothing happens in this world without
all three: HEART - WILL - RISK

JUNE 24

Passion is hard work.

Passion requires that we show up like never before.

While all great works have had someone
willing to show up in unprecedented ways,
passionately engaging will transform your
experience with your work.

"If there was one shift you might make today,
that would change your experience with your work,

What might that be?"

JUNE 25

Change of pace is crucial for long-term sustainability.

Anything pushed too hard and for too long,
takes on the substance of tough meat.
Stringy without much flavour.

Timing, and ebb and flow rather,
creates a life of relevance and refreshment.
Something all our lives can do well with.

JUNE 26

Extraordinary

What do you count as extraordinary?

And are you following others extraordinary,
Or making your own.

JUNE 27

Leading from our strengths requires that
we know our strengths.

Remaining in our strengths requires that we
know the back-side of our strengths.

There is a place where every good thing
once over-applied becomes a liability.

Make sure to know yours.

JUNE 28

While "Discretion is the better part of wisdom",
"Life and death is in the power of the tongue".

Professionalism exponentially increases with
even small changes to the quality and content
of your speech.

Here like no other place does the truth apply:
"You reap what you sow"

Sow wisely, speak wisely.

JUNE 29

Living life from the inside
out is something all of us are doing.

We may think we are hiding what is inside,
we may think no one can see us, but we are
all far more visible than we know.

Every reaction and decision
and mannerism points to the inner you.

So forget about outward grooming, get the inner core
figured out and the rest will fall into place from there.

Thoughts

JUNE 30

Taking time to ask the big questions,
Staying in those spaces of reflection and inquiry,
Habitually and consistently over time,
Will reveal itself.

New strengths,
Powerful decisions,
Solid directions.

July

TAKING ONE / DAY AT A TIME

JULY 1

Our commitments determine our destinations.

Our commitments reflect
how far we are willing to engage,
And to what extent we are willing to 'go after the gold'.

What is the gold in your life,
and what are you doing to get it?

JULY 2

The things others say about you,
Cannot touch one whit of who you are.

The things you say about others,
Touches through every layer of your entire being,
And loudly declares who you are.

Be very careful with your words.

JULY 3

Mistakes not acknowledged are mistakes
not forgiven. To make things right we must be
willing to admit what's gone wrong.

Bringing it into the light:
Simple acknowledgment, nothing morose or overdone,
Sets us up for freedom inside and out.

JULY 4

To rise above our current coping mechanisms,
Our current habits of thought and action and
interaction,

To rise above our old way and to go after a new way,

We must be intentional.

Come up with a plan, think ahead, and follow through.

JULY 5

We avoid new commitments
because we believe ourselves to be maxed out.

We feel overworked, under-valued, and on the edge.

What we are missing is that new strengths
come only when old muscles are broken down
forcing new muscles to grow.

New levels of commitment feel
like death . . . and are death.

But until we make them,
we will never know new strengths.

All we will ever know is a life
that is safe, and calculated and controlled.

And afraid, and suspicious, and pinched.

Thoughts

JULY 6

At the onset of anything much effort is required.

Once the work of intention is past the work
of 'feet to the pavement' begins.

Here we need a game
plan with small achievable goals.

One by one, bit by bit, success building on success.

JULY 7

The habit of keeping short accounts
ensures that nothing ever goes awry for too long.

Keeping up with offences and possible offences
protects the long-term standing of much of what
we are about.

Airing differences and what is non-negotiable
are habits that invest in the long-term of our lives.

Keeping short accounts is long-term investment.

JULY 8

Our passions and gifting
showed up when we were young,

Albeit often raw and immature,
but there nonetheless.

And the confirmation of our lives today
can be found in those immaturity's of youth.

What was a key characteristic of the childish you?
How is this translating into passion and gifting today?

Celebrate and give thanks for that.

JULY 9

When it doesn't go quite how
you had planned, how do you respond?

Keep in mind that there
is usually a 'win' out of most everything.

Willing to shift our perspective and look at
the growth and maturity we are really wanting,
nothing grows us like difficulty.

So, next time it doesn't go as smoothly as
planned, as perfectly as imagined,

Take it as a win.

Take the maturity offered. You won't be sorry.

JULY 10

[Half-price Frappuccino]

So says the sign at Starbucks.

What might we give away,

Without guilt, without expectations,
Simply because.

JULY 11

Leaps in forward
movement often catch us by surprise.

Long drawn-out waiting periods
often shift dramatically with rapid
development and exponential increase.

Something we are all longing for and waiting on,
and yet when it comes, can we handle it?

What strengths of heart might you require
when navigating bounty?

Acquire those now and you'll be well
set for the increase.

JULY 12

What are you looking for?

What do you want?

How might you get there?

Leave the questions open,
Don't rush to answer them,
Allow them to percolate.

The power of questions is not in having
the answers, It is in allowing the inquiry.

JULY 13

Every single group, organization, corporation,
and more has hidden codes of conduct.

Standards that are in fact the governing body.

Can you list the core values of the places
where you work and volunteer and engage?

Do you care?

JULY 14

Transitions are some
of the hardest things to navigate.

In fact, they are so difficult that many
organizations hire experts to specifically
help bridge the gap.

Yet the opportunities in times
of transition are stunning.

While the unknown is scary as heck,
there is no other time to make profound
leaps of thought and life, as during
times of transition.

If you can stand the stretching you
will come out so much stronger on the other side.

JULY 15

Our days can get away on us.

Without a plan that harnesses our best
efforts we can feel a bit lost.

Chaos can step in, in seemingly moments.

A great question in the midst of these times,
"Where am I getting called out for lack of integrity
and follow-through?"

Answering this, responding and setting
things right immediately reclaims order
out of the chaos, and immediately reclaims
creative energy for our days.

We aren't quite so lost.

JULY 16

Work Hard,

Rest Hard,

Play Hard.

Which one are you best at?

Which one are you worst at?

Which one do you disdain the most?

JULY 17

Each of us have things in the backs of our minds.

Ideas and hopes and dreams,
Often tucked away and barely acknowledged,
But nonetheless there.

In case you are waiting on someone's permission . . .
Today, simply give yourself the permission,
And unpack those dusty boxes.

JULY 18

Rare are those individuals
who are really there for others.

Who show up fully engaged,
Holding deliberate spaces,
For the best of others to be revealed,
Drawn forth,
Wooed and invited.

Yet we all do well with a bit of wooing,
Is there someone you might woo today?

Thoughts

JULY 19

Expectations are difficult to handle,
and they are even more difficult when
they are unspoken.

Setting each other up for failure
is never a good thing to do.

Rather, heading forward into
difficult conversations sets us all up for success.

For no matter which way it all turns out
we've been dealt with, and in turn deal with
others, openly and honestly.

Just one of the basic ways
of extending dignity to each other.

JULY 20

Strengths over-applied,
quickly become weaknesses,
especially in times of stress.

If you are elegantly quiet,
you may completely fade into the background.

If you are a fearless fighter,
you may swing at anyone and everyone.

The trick at all times:
Don't let your strengths get the better of you.

Thoughts

JULY 21

Authority - often considered
to be about keeping and protecting,
About walls and 'because I said so'.

Truly grows up, truly matures,
When it becomes about blessing and releasing.

JULY 22

Are you an artist, engineer or organizer?

The artist works in an eclectic style and pace.

The organizer, in direct contrast,
works in linear lines with structured methods.

The engineer takes the best of both
and makes things happen.

It doesn't matter which you are.

There is none more right or wrong than
the other. It is simply important to settle
into and give yourself the permission,

To fully be the one you are.

JULY 23

Tested,
Tried,
And True.

Are You?

JULY 24

Take every chance you get,
Grab hold of every opportunity,
To release old bitterness', old envy, old hurts.

The energy required to carry these things
creates untold strain and loss on every
other part of life.

Something none of us can afford.

Your life deserves better.

Thoughts

JULY 25

Are you sure of your angle?

When heading in a direction, that direction
must be fine-tuned and calibrated just right.

Because your final destination is simply the
sum-total of an angle exponentially worked out
and through many years.

One degree off may not seem much at the start,
but take that one degree over twenty or thirty years,
and you've arrived in a completely different place.

Ensure your aim is accurate
and you'll get where you want to go.

JULY 26

You've got a goal and have a plan.
What is the infrastructure necessary
to carry that plan?

Like a bridge that must have pilings driven
deep into the river, infrastructure is without
a doubt the most difficult part of any work.

Yet investing deeply in the front end of any works
long before anyone else recognizes that a work
has begun, ensures the goal sticks, is realized,
and lasts the test of time.

JULY 27

That space between projects
and tasks, no matter how small or short,
Is the perfect space and time to stop and rest,
To allow deep refreshment to settle in and through.

Resting hard is the perfect
accompaniment to working hard.

JULY 28

Serving those we work with,
means coming to know them.

Taking the time to study and to learn
the key values of another is never a waste of time.

It will take us to the next level, we will be trusted,
Greater responsibility and greater authority will be ours,
If we simply take the time to care.

JULY 29

There are always any number of things that we
do not know, things we are unsure of and simply
can't foresee.

When these 'unknowns' pile up and life begins
to feel overwhelming, it's the perfect time to make
a list of what we do know.

Marking what we beyond-a-shadow-of-a-doubt
know, takes our focus off the shaky unknown
and puts us back on solid 'this I know'.

Solid footing for moving forward.

JULY 30

Some days require that
we zoom in and focus on the details.

Some days require us
to zoom out and see the big picture.

Fluid movement between the two is key.

Lose sight of the big picture
and our motivation lags.

Lose sight of the details
and everything starts to unravel.

Which might be your primary focus today?

JULY 31

To go to that next level,
We must risk more than we have risked before.

To shift into our tomorrows,
We must live deeper than we have lived before.

What is the forward movement that you would like,
And what might you risk to ensure that happens?

August

TAKING ONE DAY AT A TIME

Thoughts

TAKING ONE DAY AT A TIME

AUGUST 1

The strategy for growth is different
than the strategy for holding our own.

Each of our lives holds times
of the one and then times of the other.

Most important is knowing
which it is for you at this present time,
Then adjusting accordingly.

AUGUST 2

For expectations to be healthy it is
important to have a big-picture view of things.

Small pictures result in pinching, short-term,
and often unreasonable expectations.

Whereas big-picture expectations are much
more likely to be reasonable, doable and sustainable.

AUGUST 3

Time-frames affect decision making.

While it is tempting to base our decisions
on the short-term and the here and now,

The needs screaming at us today
will not build our long-term tomorrows.

Rather, decisions that stand the test of time
must be made with time in mind.

Stretching out our time-frames changes the calibre
of our decisions and ultimately of our lives.

Go for the long-term.

Thoughts

AUGUST 4

Double-mindedness produces nothing.

Where our thoughts and heart don't
match, where the resonance is off, there
will be no good thing.

So we either change our thoughts,
or we adjust our hearts.

AUGUST 5

The stage of life is big
Are you making full use of the space?

Thoughts

AUGUST 6

Our thinking got us to today.

If you want your tomorrows
to be any different than today,
Your thinking must change
to get you there.

AUGUST 7

Each of us embody
a certain message to our worlds.

Each of us bring a flavor
unique to us and a gift to those around.

Your life speaks.

What is it saying?

What might you like it to say?

AUGUST 8

We all have equal opportunity every
single day to make ourselves invaluable.

Here and only here is our gifting
and the truest thing we should be about.

How might you be invaluable today?

Thoughts

AUGUST 9

What are you glad for today?

Celebrate that.

AUGUST 10

Knowing what we are NOT about
and what we are NOT going to do is
as important as knowing what we are
about, what we are doing.

In fact, to continue with what we are about,
the strength to stand on our No's becomes
more and more critical.

Our NO muscle must
grow alongside our YES muscle.

AUGUST 11

Good friends are critical to life.

Who has your back?

Whose back do you have?

Invest in friends.

AUGUST 12

All professionals ask for feedback.

Knowing that measuring is the way to increasing.
Whether in relationships or business feedback
is the metric by which we know we are either
advancing or losing ground.

Those afraid of feedback will lose ground
and never know it and will be the last surprised
by it: wondering what went wrong.

The professional continues to ask in various ways,
"How was the service today? How might I serve you
better tomorrow?"

AUGUST 13

The clothes you wear tell a story.

What story are they telling?

What story do you want them to tell?

It's not so much the clothes that matter,
rather, are the clothes telling the story
of the real you?

Thoughts

AUGUST 14

Going forth with what we have,
Utilizes 'us' to the fullest measure.

Proves stamina and fortitude,
Finds strengths and resiliency's,
That have always been there.

AUGUST 15

New habits are best acquired one at a time.

There is nothing worse than setting ourselves
up for failure because we are trying to establish
too many things at once.

One new thing every six months results
in twelve new things five years down the road.

Establish one thing at a time
and you are well set-up for success.

AUGUST 16

Effort is heart + will + risk.

Many have the heart,
Some have the will,
And even fewer will risk.

If you were to increase any one of these
at this time, how might your effort be impacted?

Thoughts

AUGUST 17

Our vision solidly placed on the goal
sees past the rocks and the obstacles in our path.

Therefore:

First - Keep your head up,

Second - Don't look down,

Third - Focus on the finish line,

Fourth - Give it all you've got,

Fifth & Final - Enjoy the win.

Thoughts

TAKING ONE DAY AT A TIME

AUGUST 18

It is always a good time to count our blessings

What are we truly thankful?

What truly enriches our lives?

Give thanks today.

AUGUST 19

In order for muscles to become
strong the fibres must first break down.

What part of your life or business
is breaking down in order to become stronger?

Even more strategic: What part of your life
or business might you break down in order
to become stronger?

AUGUST 20

Where might you take initiative today?

How might that influence your days to come?

What difference might it make to those around you?

Take some initiative today.

AUGUST 21

Blame and fault finding strips us of our power.

Every time we leave the blame with
someone else we have just diminished our power.

Stepping into 100%
responsibility, restores us to full power,

Something we can't afford to do without.

AUGUST 22

What have you forgotten lately,
and what is your response once you realize?

Shame has us pretending it didn't happen
and hoping no one noticed.

But forgetting is never really about anyone
else, what they think or don't think, whether
they noticed or not.

It's always about us.

What do we think and how do we respond?

Which is really about the way we want to be in the
world. How do you want to be in the world?

Answer this question and the how's and whys
of going forward in the midst of what you've
forgotten will answer themselves.

AUGUST 23

What moves us? What moves you?

Action is always
the response to something that moves us.

Do you know, are you aware, of what moves you?

And what is that movement about?

Answer this and you will
come to know yourself a little bit better.

Answer this and you will come to find if what moves
you is what you really want to be moved by.

Maybe it's time to take it up a notch.

Maybe it's time to be more
intentional about where you put your feet.

What moves you?

AUGUST 24

We all have only so much social equity.

Much like money in the bank,
our social equity has a beginning and an end.

And we must decide how we are using this
social equity, in what order and to what extent
and for what exactly.

Most importantly we don't want to waste
our social equity. We don't want to squander
it or abuse it.

Social equity is to be handled carefully,
understood intelligently, and managed wisely.

AUGUST 25

Moving forward requires a few things:

1. Clear vision about the end-line—What is the goal? How does it smell and taste? What are the emotions of the vision?

   Who are you once you reach the end-line?

2. Specific clarity about the end-line—What exactly is the goal?

Imagine six dynamics or realities tied into the end-line goal, which one is really the point?

If a dynamic was left out and missed the most, which one is it?

Answer these questions and the details of your days will begin to flow much easier and more naturally.

AUGUST 26

No longer is our world so much
about what we are doing but about
what and who we are.

Who we are determines our 'doing',
not the other way around.

The most amazing question to ask,

"Who do I want to be in the world?"
"How might I move through my days?"

Picture that, picture you; who do you see?
What do you see?

In your mind's eye practice it up, change
it around, mix and match until who you want
to be is congruent with you are.

Powerful intention always ends in powerful results.

Thoughts

AUGUST 27

Integrity starts in the details of life.

So to do our self-destructive tendencies.

Looking to avoid all that is 'great' or 'wow'
about us, we can let the details of life slip.

Playing less-than never helped anyone,
least of all yourself.

Pay attention to those details.

They will tell you how you are feeling about life.

AUGUST 28

The more important our work
the greater the dichotomies grow.

The greater the work the greater
our sense of smallness.

The quaking is a good sign,
it means you are on to something.

But it requires that you engage
a level deeper than previously managed.

It requires that you become less, taking
a back seat to the work, to the influence,
and to the impact.

The more important your work
the less it is about you.

AUGUST 29

To engage:

- to partner with

- to advocate for

- to support with all of one's heart,
   mind, spirit and body

  - to arrange one's life around

  - to make decisions based on

  - to take into account

Who and what are you engaging today?

And how might you up the ante and engage even more?

AUGUST 30

The work once difficult becomes easy.
The tasks once out of reach become common-place.
The effort once required eases off and lessens.
The passion once required becomes less.

Apathy sets in.

Bewilderment takes hold.

What was once fun becomes boring.

Same old, same old.

The only way out of this is to risk.
Risk to take on something new.
Risk to stretch into a fresh place.

That place where we head
back to novice to begin again.

Where work, tasks, effort
and passion take hold once more.

AUGUST 31

Powerful mixes come when we
give our lives over to something bigger than us.

Playing it safe rarely produces anything of worth.

The 'bigger than us' place requires profound humility,
and that rock-solid sense of who we are; it is a sense
of self that can't be lost nor taken away.

Invest in who you are in the world, simply
that the world might be profoundly blessed
by who you are.

September

TAKING ONE DAY AT A TIME

Thoughts

SEPTEMBER 1

Finding our center is more about
our inner circumstance, rather than our outer.

The tasks and to-do's of our days
will always be more than time allows.

Yet in the midst we
can decide how to move and have our being.

Who do we want to be in the world?

In what manner might
we move through our days?

SEPTEMBER 2

Timing is one of the
most critical elements to our lives.

Push something to happen before its time
and we merely have lots of effort without much fruit.

Delay and hold back when the time
is right and we miss opportunity and doors shut.

It is its own art-form to recognize that 'right' time.

Most importantly:

- Be ready

- Pay close attention

- Be ready

- Then move nimbly

SEPTEMBER 3

Transitions are never easy.

We find ourselves caught
off guard and oft-times back at novice.

We thought we had it together (and we did and do),
but coming up to something brand new always
leaves us as though we are starting again.

And while it doesn't feel
nice, this is absolutely necessary.

It means there are parts of the world to
be experienced and explored that are fresh
and new, and this is where that sense
of being alive enters in.

No longer are we bored.

SEPTEMBER 4

Have to love those unexpected moments when
someone surprises you with the simplest of regard.

- Your teenage daughter asks you how your day went

- A friend texts to ask how they might
  support you this day

- Email from a colleague expressing
  commitment to be there

It doesn't take much to
make a difference in someone's day.

How might you show the simplest of regard today?

Thoughts

SEPTEMBER 5

We are all made of heart, mind, spirit, and body.

Which of these do you nurture the most?

And which of these could use a bit more investment?

Which are you most comfortable with?

And which are most afraid of?

Hint: The one most uncomfortable is the one to focus on. Till it's not scary anymore.

SEPTEMBER 6

What are you building?

It is important to know the scope
of the work and to be settled in that.

Not trying to make apples, oranges,
Or oranges, apples.

Just make those apples
the best apples they can be.

The same goes for the oranges.

SEPTEMBER 7

What is the work?

In every job and business, career,
and upstart, it is incredibly easy to be doing
busywork and not the actual work that will
make a difference to your bottom-line.

What part of the work you are doing?

What part of the work might you do
that would make the biggest difference?

SEPTEMBER 8

Consistency is key.

Regardless of what the consistency is,
nothing else supports (or denies) our integrity
more than the ability for others to trust us.

If you do nothing else, make some small
yet profound tweaks in areas of consistency.

It'll make a difference, guaranteed.

SEPTEMBER 9

Complacency is the death of us.

Where are you complacent?

How might you overcome complacency?

What would change if you did?

Thoughts

TAKING ONE DAY / AT A TIME

SEPTEMBER 10

Watching and waiting for
that new opportunity requires a few things.

1. We know the essence of what we are looking for.

2. We clearly know the key components we are
   NOT looking for.

3. We hold it all with open hands.

At that point we are
prepared for opportunity to show up.

SEPTEMBER 11

Before taking that next step
it is important to list all the requirement of self.

Requirements of one's time, energy, the specific tasks,
and even more importantly, the integral values and
motivations, must be assessed.

The values and motivations are the key.
For if they are in place time and energy
take care of themselves.

SEPTEMBER 12

All goals are better managed broken
down into bits and worked one at a time.

Focus on one major goal every six months
and within two years you will have four major
things happening and in sync.

It's a much better plan than trying for two years
to establish four new major goals at one time
and ending up with nothing accomplished.

Thoughts

SEPTEMBER 13

Waiting is one of the hardest things to do,
especially in the face of expectations and goals.

Yet waiting is often a refining
factor in our stamina and character.

Stamina and character must be present
to successfully walk forward in whatever
you are waiting on.

And while short-cuts are for short-term
thinking, sticking through the wait grants
long-term substance and strength.

If in doubt, always go for the character development.

SEPTEMBER 14

Internal preparations are just
as important as the external ones.

Maybe even more so.

Don't discount the time taken for internal
shifts to happen. For the work done behind
the scenes creates stability and solidness
long before anything 'real' shows up.

Invest in your own internal prep.

SEPTEMBER 15

The best work comes from deep inside us.

And it is something we avoid at all costs.

We would rather keep busy with this and that.
Yet arranging our work and preparing the work
is not the same thing as doing the work.

Although these things sure feel good at the
time they disguise our true impact and the true
scope of influence.

What might your great work be?

SEPTEMBER 16

One of the ways to ensure
we are doing the work that matters,

Is to refuse to do the work that doesn't matter.

We only have so much attention to give,
To what are we giving it?

The greatest satisfactions come from doing less
and doing the little more deliberately.

Thoughts

SEPTEMBER 17

Recently heard about a fellow stating that he
hated his schooling, the topic held no interest,
and required no passion.

And yet he kept pursuing the same line of study.

How easy it is to sell ourselves
short with work that does not inspire.

While the discipline to stick to it and to finish
what we start has its place, these things are little
comfort in the face of life passing us by.

Choose work that requires your very guts,
and become an inspiration.

SEPTEMBER 18

The best solutions are often
the result of plans not going as planned.

We think 'Plan A' with much enthusiasm.

But what if there were no Plan A, what is Plan B?

Hint: Plan B is always better than Plan A

So go for that one.

SEPTEMBER 19

There are always solutions out of sight.

Just around from the corner
of our vision are all sorts of answers.

We simply need the clarity and perspective
that is bigger than our present way of thinking.

But first we need to be open
to different new and bigger thinking.

Do we really want answers and solutions?

And what might we have to give up to get them?

SEPTEMBER 20

Your difficulties are saving you if you let them.

Left to our own devices we
would have everything pretty and perfect.

But the real trans-formative work deep inside
us would go undone, and while life would
have a veneer it wouldn't be real.

Hint: go for the real and let the veneer crumble away.

SEPTEMBER 21

Recharging is all about making a shift, taking a time out, and shaking up the normal for just a touch of time.

It doesn't take a lot to recharge. Just a bit of time will often do. But it does take commitment to make it happen.

Recharging does not just happen all on its own. We must be the masters of it.

How do you recharge, and how might you plan a bit more recharging into your life this week?

SEPTEMBER 22

Grieving - a necessary investment.

We generally don't understand
the privilege of grieving available to us.

With relative ease we have more affordability
in terms of time and focus and energy for grieving,
than ever available in previous times.

How might you take advantage of the
privilege of grieving and invest in your inner health.

You will free up a bounty of energy for other things.

Grieving - a great investment

Thoughts

SEPTEMBER 23

Self-care is highly underrated and yet highly important.

Without self-care we decline in emotional,
spiritual, and physical health.

Fact is the better a person is at self-care,
the higher the success of that person.

Like the wheels on a car that need
regular alignment, we require the same.

Align your emotions, your spiritual equilibrium,
and your physical health to the highest possible
frequency and everything else will take on new
clarity and energy.

How might you invest in some self-care this week?

SEPTEMBER 24

The thinking that got us
to today will not take us to tomorrow.

The paradigms that got us to today
won't get us to the future we are envisioning.

In your mind's eye what about
your future is different than today?

And in your mind what of your thinking
has to change to ensure that different tomorrow?

Today's thinking won't get you there.

Invest in new thinking,
and you'll get that new tomorrow.

SEPTEMBER 25

Reaping what we sow, judgments are the worst.

Looking at our lives we can usually see clear
evidence of our judgments coming back to bite us.

What in your life is less than satisfactory?

Trace it back, do you find a judgment
about that very thing somewhere in your past?

Let the judgments go and begin
to receive a better future.

SEPTEMBER 26

The emotional frequency of your desires
determines whether it comes your way or not.

Meaning, if you are planning and creating
and investing in that thing you want, but your
emotions are not in sync, if your emotions
are negative while your desire is positive,
guess which wins out?

The emotions.

They trump every other effort in our lives
and determine the true results of all our investments.

Change your emotions around your
goals and see your goals begin to fall into place.

SEPTEMBER 27

Our bodies carry the strain of our lives,
the weight of our losses, and the heaviness
of the years.

Invest in some deep inner care
and have your whole being lightened.

Gone is the strain, gone is the weight,
gone is the heaviness.

You won't believe the difference.

What might you do with all that new energy?

SEPTEMBER 28

The personal infrastructure of integrity and habits
and follow-through must be in place before the
greatest works of our lives begin.

So too are the free structures of faith
and stamina and resilience necessary to
carry the weight of these greatest works.

Greatest works are available to all of us
and we prove we are ready for them by our
faithfulness to the lesser works.

The very places where integrity, habits,
follow-through, faith, stamina, and resilience
are formed and proven.

Thoughts

SEPTEMBER 29

Work is a core expression of our lives.

   What are you working at?

   What might you be working at?

   How might you be working at it?

But most important,
what is the real work within the work?

Find this and work, will take on new
satisfaction, power and significance in your life.

It all starts to make sense.

SEPTEMBER 30

Traditional wisdom insists we take on only
what we can handle, what we are capable of,
and what seems manageable.

The problem is, this formula is based on us
on our own and by ourselves.

It defies the place of working in collaboration
with others and engaging work and influence
that matters most.

We are better together.

And the way to 'better together' is by entering
into something bigger than us, broader than what
we can manage on our own, with more scope than,
on our own, we are capable.

Forget manageable, go for collaborations
where many hands make light work.

October

TAKING ONE DAY AT A TIME

OCTOBER 1

There is a wall that stands between
what is manageable and what is beyond
our 'on our own' capabilities.

It is a big wall, high and wide and deep.

Getting over it requires that you see something
that inspires you, action that moves you, and guts
that require everything in you.

Not many make it, but those who do are privileged
to energy like they never had before, community
that they only dreamed of, and strength to go farther
longer and deeper.

Over the wall is an amazing place.

The key: Invest your time and
efforts in something that is bigger than yourself.

Lose yourself and you will find life.

Simple and scary as that.

OCTOBER 2

Runners know the wall of fatigue and
physical desperation, the sense of needing
to give up and of not going farther.

That invisible barrier that stands in the way
to increased energy and that sense of being
able to run forever without ever tiring out.

Runners also know they can break through that wall.
In life it is the same. The wall makes us believe we only
have so much energy, so much time, and so
much ability to put into each day.

On the other side of the wall, energy
is compounded, time falls away, and ability
is leveraged into something so much more.

Hint: get over the wall. Invest in something
bigger than you.

OCTOBER 3

The voices warning us of the wall are many.

"Don't do too much."

"You will burn out."

"It isn't safe."

Just to name a few.

Getting over the wall requires you
ignore the threats, kick off the worries of others,
and take a few bold moves on your own.

Once over the wall, there is a whole community
waiting. But that climb and final kick over the wall,
that is yours to do.

Thoughts

OCTOBER 4

Every once in a while we
must look at what we are doing.

Why we are doing it?

How we are doing it?

What might we do to make it better?

It's not an easy process and it takes some
time to come to full clarity and direction but all
query is well worth the process.

Ask the right kinds of questions, open up
the paradigms, and shift into the next stage
of development. You won't remain the same.

OCTOBER 5

If you are building a team of any sort make
sure to find people who have experienced at
least one big failure.

For those who have failed are often:

- Wise beyond their years

- Carrying a mark of humility critical to team success

- Compassionate and truly invested in people

Those who have known
failure are the best kind of people.

Stay away, stay far away, from the perfect ones.

OCTOBER 6

We are only as strong as the people around us.

The team and your
colleagues are critical to your success.

What kind of people are they?

What type of people do they need to be?

What style of person are you missing?

And how might you go about gathering
more of the right kind of people around you?

OCTOBER 7

It is an art to know when
to hold course and when to change track.

Wait too long to change
track and we miss opportunity,

Move too fast and we are pushing a huge stone uphill.

That thing you are considering:

What three things will tell
you that the timing is just right?

OCTOBER 8

It is the perfect time to map out some
goals and objectives for the months to come.

What three things would you like
to have completed six months from now?

In those same six months what two
ways might you create an impact in your reality?

And what one new habit might you establish?

Thoughts

TAKING ONE DAY AT A TIME

OCTOBER 9

When we want to make changes it works best
to break the changes down into manageable bites.

For large focus shifts requiring work habit
and lifestyle changes it works best to work
at those a month at a time.

Instead of shifting four areas this month focus
on one shift every month or so, and in six months
you will be farther ahead than if you tried to
make all those changes at once.

OCTOBER 10

Increasingly so we become aware that
within our difficulties and problems, are in
fact the solutions to the next phase of our life.

Everything has a silver lining.

Quite simply we must be open to finding it,
to seeing it, and to allowing it into our life.

Do we want the problem,
or do we want the silver lining?

We can't have both.

OCTOBER 11

When faced with two opposites, the farthest ends
of two extremes, we have more choices than we realize.

While we tend to think of extremes as opposite
poles on a continuum (and they are), what we don't
realize is that a line can be made into a circle.

The two opposing ends of any reality
can be brought around to meet each other.

We need not move one way or the other.

It is not all or not.

What if it was both/and rather than either/or?

Bring two opposing forces together and find
solutions and new ways of doing things; solutions
that are stronger than that found at either
end of a continuum.

Thoughts

OCTOBER 12

Perspective is everything.

Are we expecting good things, or failure?

Are we working towards solutions,
or relishing in the drama of problems?

Do our actions reflect forward movement,
or are we shutting down possibility?

Do our attitudes celebrate, or complain?

Perspective, it is everything.

OCTOBER 13

Managing our time is in fact, not so much
about time but about focus ability and energy.

Instead of asking, "Do I have the time?",
ask, "Do I have the energy?"

Projects, new endeavours, shifts in tasks and
schedules, has more to do with energy than time.

Everything we do takes different amounts of energy.
And every new thing we do takes the lions share.

Therefore, whenever we begin something
new, it is good to ask ourselves, "What can I put
aside for a time, to ensure I have the energy for
this new thing?"

OCTOBER 14

While difficulties press on us, flatten us out
for a time and always seem to draw from us
more than we have to give, they also pave the
way for the new and the better.

Through the valley's of 'death' when it
seems all is on the chopping block are actually
opportunities in disguise.

We just have to hang through the hardship,
embrace the process, and grieve the losses.

OCTOBER 15

In grieving we are prepared to take on the new and go after fresh visions. We will look back one day and see that we were changed for the better.

We grew, acquired new perspectives, had our hearts opened in new ways, and if we had our choice wouldn't go back to who we were before.

It is a process to be sure.

And while certainly not
a nice process always a good one.

Thoughts

OCTOBER 16

Waiting: It seems to take forever.

Yet there are a good many
things we can do in the waiting.

How might we prepare for what is to come?

What might we invest in while we wait?

Are there any specifics
to focus on while we have the time?

Who shall we journey alongside during this time?

Use the waiting in your life as a leverage
to the things you've always wanted and imagined.

Thoughts

OCTOBER 17

The journey's of our lives are well
planned sequences of growth and development.

While we don't understand it all, and some of it
certainly don't like, if we take a step back and open
up the lens on our life, we will see that it is not
quite so random as we might have thought.

Embracing the journey past enables us to embrace
the journey forward; trusting the process of our days
frees us to relish in the process of our days.

OCTOBER 18

What are you thankful for today?

Gratitude grounds us in strength
and motivates us forward.

Make habits of gratitude each and every day.

- Five things you loved today

- Three things you are expecting tomorrow

- Two people who blessed you this week

Gratitude stretches our
hearts and eases in happy expectations.

The rest begins to fall into place.

Thoughts

OCTOBER 19

Every single one of us has
full opportunity to make ourselves invaluable.

Where we work, where we volunteer, in our families
and our homes; how might you be invaluable today?

What would it take?

What is one shift you might make to become
invaluable to those around you?

Invaluable, we make a difference everywhere we go.

Our lives are changed and so are other's.

OCTOBER 20

Life doesn't always go as planned.

When things aren't what we expect our 'buttons' are often pushed and old lies surface and default make-shift solutions come to the fore.

Head into all these things straight on, slaying them left and right, allowing none to stand.

Everyone is not out to get you. God doesn't hate you. And no, this is not punishment for something from your eighth grade year.

Take a breath, push the pause button for a bit, step back, look at the big picture, say 'no' to the lies, and ask yourself, "How might this be the best thing that ever happened to me?"

Thoughts

OCTOBER 21

Each and every one of us bring
something of great beauty simply in who we are.

But in order for it to show we
must participate in an unveiling of sorts.

Where we put aside the risk
of 'exposure' for the joy of mutual blessing.

Where we step out of self-protection
and put it on the line in service to others.

Only then, does the great beauty
of you make the impact it is meant to make.

OCTOBER 22

Change, progress and forward
movement doesn't happen in a vacuum.

We are unable to shift
and leverage into the new all on our own.

It takes others around us, the voices of many
speaking into our lives, both encouraging us
and blessing us.

If you are feeling discouraged or stuck,
confounded and unmotivated, it is probably
time for a few good conversations with those
who have your back and are invested in you.

OCTOBER 23

Every day has new things,
new perspectives, and new strengths.

This day is perfect for your strengthening,
perfect for perspectives of comfort
and understanding beyond what you have known,

And those new things - may they bless your
socks off -

Watch for these today.

Thoughts

OCTOBER 24

Reaching forward has us
stretching beyond our present capacity.

Just like lifting weights at the gym new strengths
come only as old muscle is broken down and replaced
with new muscle.

Where do you need new muscle today?

Don't be afraid to let the old break down, it's the
only way to new strength and increased capacity.

OCTOBER 25

Waiting has got to be one of the most difficult things in life. In our fast-baked culture we want speed and have lost the ability to pause and to rest in the wait.

But it is here in the wait that we learn a 'rest' over our souls that cannot come in the hurry.

There are lessons in the wait that cannot be learned in activity.

If 'waiting' is your current season know that this is the time for deep personal infrastructure to be strengthened and solidified.

Hurry can't accomplish this work.

Thoughts

OCTOBER 26

'Without a vision the people perish'

What can you see and what can you not see?

Making things happen is all about having
a picture, a vision and a goal.

If we can't see it we can't make it happen.

If we can't envision it it won't come to be.

And if you can't see on your own
gather others around you who will help you see.

Your life depends on it.

Thoughts

OCTOBER 27

Most of the time it is best to be
cooperative and as accommodating as we can be.

But there are other times when we need to be the wall.

The Wall is the backbone of your non-negotiables.

There are many things that we are better
off without. And when it is unwise to be cooperative
or accommodating, simply imagine yourself as
The Wall.

Be the wall.

Thoughts

OCTOBER 28

Transitions are only possible in the context of stability.

There must be a base of constancy
in order for change to happen.

Therefore, invest in stability and constancy.

If for no other reason that life might
be free to shift and transition to greater freedom.

Thoughts

OCTOBER 29

Time outs are as beneficial
for adults as for kids. Perhaps more so!

The need to recharge and to refresh only
becomes more paramount as our responsibilities
and influence increase.

What refreshes you most?

And how might you recharge today?

OCTOBER 30

What is your relationship with trust?

If 'Trust' were a person
how do you feel about him or her?

It is hard if not impossible to accomplish
anything of worth without trust being an integral
piece in the mix.

Building trust, both what we need to trust
and what others need from us for trust, are
elements we are wise to understand
and then build.

How might you increase trust today?

OCTOBER 31

Excellence opens many doors.

When faced with seemingly impossible tasks
take the time to learn anything and everything
you can, to assist with that task.

The bigger the task the deeper the equipping.

The more important the task the longer the learning.

When faithful with little we will be entrusted with much.

Find excellence in the little tasks then prepare
to move on to excellence in bigger tasks.

November

TAKING ONE DAY AT A TIME

NOVEMBER 1

Another day is asking us,
'What might you do with me?'

While every day has its routine and ordinary,
the tasks and responsibilities of every other day,
Maybe today is a day to engage something a little
more 'out there'.

Maybe today is the day that
something extraordinary plants a seed.

And maybe today is the day where years
of routine and ordinary converge together,
giving way to something more than ordinary.

What might you make of today?

What might today have for you?

NOVEMBER 2

When things go sour and we lose our focus,
make mistakes and miss deadlines, the best
thing to do is to pick ourselves up from the dust,
brush off and carry on.

With our humility heightened, our pride set aside,
and our focus determined to set things right, we
just might make a bigger impact and different kinds
of decisions than before the fail.

Quality of life and business and ministry
doesn't depend solely on the good and up times
but depends just as much on the clarity that
comes out of the mistakes.

Harness it all.

Discount nothing.

Make use of every piece.

And go forward.

NOVEMBER 3

In order to climb the mountains
we must not be afraid of the depths.

For the capacity of heart
and mind found in the deep places,
Breaks open our hearts to contain
greater things to come,
To handle the air at great heights.

Without the difficulty,
Expect no glory

NOVEMBER 4

'Yea though I walk through the shadow of death . . . '

The shadows of death once walked
through bring us more clarity than ever before.

Much of what we thought was important we find out
isn't. Perhaps not sure about our strength before we
are now. And what may have been buried dreams
take on visible importance.

No matter the kind of death, a loved one, a marriage,
a business, or a dream, coming through on the other
side has us with gifts and strengths and wisdom that
we never would have had but for the death.

And while death is never
the goal it always leads to life.

If we let it.

NOVEMBER 5

It takes a breaking down of our
inner constructs to build new strengths.

In order to take on fresh perspectives,
we must be willing to cast off the old.

Thing is, we are emotionally married
to our old perspectives and our inner constructs.

The 'building' of you and I has gotten us this far,
but our lives are outstripping the building.

So do we simply keep decorating and
redecorating with little renovations here or there?

Or do we go with a gut job,
start from scratch, and build forward?

NOVEMBER 6

Giving over old ways for new ways is not easy.

The most painful things to trade in are our successes.

Where we have already 'figured it out'
are often the very places we become stuck.

Perhaps we can't imagine anything
different or better. Perhaps we are afraid to try.

NOVEMBER 7

We all live with a lot of equations that we firmly hold,
that we depend on, and that we order our lives around.

And we can tell the quality of our equations
by the quality of our life. We can tell the stage
of our life by the equations we live by.

Do our equations reflect life and bounty
and freedom or do they reflect fear and suspicion
and less-than?

Listen to your language. For the next week pay
attention to the words coming out of your mouth,
the attitudes of your heart behind the words,
and the tenor or tone of emotions within them.

You just may learn a lot and you may
find some equations that can be done away with.

NOVEMBER 8

We are all governed by our thoughts.

But our thoughts are different.

Every strata and sub-culture
has its own thought and language.

For instance, the blue collar sector has a very specific
way of thinking and the white collar sector has a very
specific way of thinking.

Hint: they are completely different ways of thinking.
Nothing wrong with either one as long as its where
you want to be.

If it's not where you want
to be, change your thinking first.

The rest will then follow along naturally.

NOVEMBER 9

Forward progress is always bit by bit.

We are rarely taken from
point C to point Q in one big swoop.

But when we are, we can be sure that the
internal work to carry such a shift has been
happening for some time.

Just as much as looking for and engaging and
asking for big movements is the preparedness
within ourselves.

Both are as key as the other; invest in both.

Thoughts

NOVEMBER 10

Sometimes we just know.

We know who we are to marry, who will be
alongside for the long haul, the career best for us,
and the general tenor of our lives.

We know.

And then other times, we have no clue. Can't tell
what will be next year even, aren't sure of the next
step after this one and are just as expectant as
everyone else as to the tenor of our life as it unfolds.

And most times we have mixes of both of these.

Things we clearly know and other things we
simply must journey to and through in order to know.

Neither is more right nor wrong than the other. The trick
is to trust our guts, go with what we know, and venture
forth in spite of what we don't know.

NOVEMBER 11

Growth is a constant process of reinventing ourselves.

Where we take who we have always been,
and examine and determine what is useful to stay,
and what is better to go.

Not all of who we are is static.

Much of it are mindsets and paradigms that,
while they may have worked for some time, won't
often take us forward to where we want to be.

The good news: we can engage a change of mind,
and different way of thinking and responding, acting
and reacting. Our expectations can be richer
and more dynamic than ever before.

Reinventing ourselves takes intentionality
but is not outside the scope of any one of us.

What about yourself, might you reinvent this week?

Thoughts

NOVEMBER 12

One of the premier abilities of those who
succeed big is the ability to zoom way out
and see the big picture.

Take in years at a time, see the full scope, make
decisions for the long term, and understand the
minute in context of the years.

The other complementary ability is then taking
that camera lens, zooming into the details, the to-do
list of years and months and weeks, days and hours.

Focusing on what must be done today and what
will really make a difference in the long run is the
work of each and every day.

Focus out to big picture
goals and focus in to today's tasks.

NOVEMBER 13

When we know the next few things we must
get done it is wise to alert those around us of the
focus reminding that we won't be available per
usual and generally mark off the hours necessary
to stay on task.

We then take ourselves in hand sometimes
by the scruff of our collars and get to it.

Stay with the task, keep the primary focus (all
other focus' will have their day), doggedly pursue
the work, until it is done.

Take a break.
Reconnect with those in your world.
Pause, and then repeat.

You'll be amazed how much can be accomplished.

NOVEMBER 14

It is often the case that in order to get
a project done we must let other projects
slide for a time.

If we are stuck on maintaining all things per usual
even when something extraordinary is on our plate,
even that extraordinary is brought down to ordinary.

Big projects leverage our strengths forward,
harness our particular genius in a new way, and
generally launch us to that next level in a way
that will never happen if we must keep
everything as usual.

Big projects, the kinds that change our life,
are not usual and should not be relegated so.

NOVEMBER 15

Do the people around us know what we are about?

Can the people around you tell,
succinctly and accurately, what you are about?

Ask every once in awhile, "What do you say I am
about?" and see what they say.

If the answers are sketchy or half-baked you know
you have a problem. You've not spoken or shared
well enough, or often enough of who you are and
what you are about.

To remedy that: every chance you get explain
once more the passion of your heart and life, how
you express that and with the particular aplomb
that is you.

If others don't know what you are really about
take it unto yourself to ensure they do.

NOVEMBER 16

When a period of hard work
is accomplished how do you celebrate?

What little (or big) response do you give yourself?

Affirmation and celebration never hurts. Ever.

How might you express your gladness today?

NOVEMBER 17

Half the world lives in 'ought' and 'should'.
The other half lives in 'opportunity' and 'initiative'.

And the difference between the two lies completely
and 100% in our thinking and attitude.

Moving from 'ought' and the 'should' and going
for the 'opportunity' and 'initiative' is all about:

First - Forgiveness - leaving the past behind

Secondly - Knowing Ourselves - self awareness
that understands what we bring to
the table

Third - Stepping Out - getting it that you are
a gift to others

Opportunity & Initiative,
it's yours to take hold of any time you want.

NOVEMBER 18

The deepest satisfactions come from
that grand mixture of the comfort of the past
and the excitement of an unknown future.

Anticipation wraps all of what we have known
and takes it forward into what we do not yet know.

Deep satisfactions do not have to know everything
in advance, they don't have to control outcomes,
and they are comfortable with ambiguity.

Become uncomfortable with the as-yet
unknown, look forward, and bring the best
of the past with you.

NOVEMBER 19

Every day begin with meditation.

Invest in introspection between yourself and God.

Silent contemplation before
action ensures our activity is focused.

While the days take off in a huff, our start
can be quiet, questioning, inviting, and curious.

It's the best way to set up your best days.

Thoughts

NOVEMBER 20

Great strength lies in the ability to make
plans, secure our passions towards an outcome,
set the future in place, and then alongside
all of that . . .

To hold it all with open hands,
to need not a bit of it to happen.

For when we stop trying to manipulate
the world the world comes round to our side.

NOVEMBER 21

Control is the opposite of freedom.

Where we must control, we are not free.

Where we must ensure, we are not free.

What new freedom are you looking for today?

And what control might you give up in that quest?

Thoughts

TAKING ONE DAY / AT A TIME

NOVEMBER 22

There are new vistas all around us.

Yet they are often on the other side of some wall.
The good news, you can get over the wall.

You can push through to something new.

Bad news, there will be many (usually those
closest to us) that are not okay with you moving
over your walls.

For all sorts of fears show
up when anything is about to change.

Good news, you can still get over the walls,
if you will just let their fears be theirs.

They are not yours. I hope you know that.

NOVEMBER 23

We have multiple unspoken rules of engagement.
In every relationship there are the 'way we do this'
woven in and around and through.

Change who you are, reinvent yourself for your future,
and the 'way we do this' will shift and change as well.

It is what is meant when we
say, "lose your life and you will find it"

Because the only way forward is in the strength
that requires nothing from others, controls nothing
about the future, and maintains an open hand in
the most fearful of times.

NOVEMBER 24

As you shift and grow and change
give those around you time to adjust.

As much as we say we want change,
we really don't. Most in fact are afraid of change.

It's why we make incremental movements
in who we are, in work and business, in passions
and callings.

Bit by bit gives those around us the time to catch up.

NOVEMBER 25

Whatever great idea you
have in mind, count the cost first.

Figure out the parameters:
how often? how long? in what way?

Secure the energy for your plan:
what will it take? who is by my side?

Then wait on the exact timing to launch,
knowing that once you start you want to continue.

Thoughts

NOVEMBER 26

Whenever we begin something that is new
to us it is important to limit the number of people
you tell it to.

Great energy must be reserved for the action
required to stick a new thing through from start
to middle to end. Don't waste that energy by
speaking too soon.

Stay in the place where you are not sure it will
all work out. Stay in the place where your focus
in on making it work out.

Keep it a secret and when there is really
something to talk about others will do the
sharing for you.

NOVEMBER 27

Everything moves along by the
power of the people alongside you.

Who is on your team?

Who do you need on your team?

What kind of person are you missing on your team?

How might you take your team to the next level?

What might that next level look like?

Whether you are a business, an organization,
or simply a person stretching to that next level,
build a team around you.

You won't be sorry.

NOVEMBER 28

Always look at anything from a number of angles.

Call in the experts, ask your friends, have a group meet.

Then, create a space of time,
sit back, and let it all percolate.

Don't discount your own gut.
(If something seems off, it usually is off)

Do the figuring, count the cost, make the
preparations,THEN - either take the plunge
or pull the plug.

Nothing need happen but what you are
seeking to make happen. Go at it with 200%
and full-on confidence.

NOVEMBER 29

The best work comes from deep inside us.

And it is something we avoid at all costs.

We would rather keep busy with this and that.
Yet arranging our work preparing the work is not the
same thing as doing the work.

Although these things sure feel good at the time
they disguise our true impact, and the true scope
of influence if we were to truly risk to produce
great work.

What might your great work be?

NOVEMBER 30

Great strength lies in the ability to make plans,
secure our passions towards an outcome, set the
future in place, and then, alongside all of that . . .

To hold it all with open hands,
to need not a bit of it to happen.

For when we stop trying to manipulate
the world the world comes round to our side.

December

TAKING ONE DAY AT A TIME

Thoughts

DECEMBER 1

What is one change in your routine
that would make a world of difference for you?

It is far too easy to carry on the same
old way with the same patterns and routines.

But what if one small shift
would make a big change for you?

Would you be willing to make that shift?

And what might it be.

DECEMBER 2

A bias toward action is what takes us forward.

Yes we must think.
We must plan.
It is prudent to gauge our movement.

But after all that we must take action.
We can't have it all perfect.

Not everything will be predicted.
There will be surprises as we go forward.

All the same a bias toward action takes us forward.

DECEMBER 3

No matter our business or career it always pays
to regularly step back and take in the big picture.

Spend some time asking questions.

Where have I come from?

How did I get here?

What might my future look like?

Envision it, jot about it, draw some pictures,
write a poem even; whatever it takes, get a creative
visual about where you are heading.

DECEMBER 4

While our world rapidly changes we must remain
aligned with principles that have stood the test of time.

Matters of trustworthiness and respect and civility,
principles of dignity and honor, are more important
now than they have ever been.

To last in a glass-bubble world
you must up your game like never before.

If you do there is not a thing to worry about.

On the other hand fear of all our worlds
rapid changes only apply to those who have
something to hide.

Give to this world trust, respect, civility,
dignity and honor, and all of this will gladly
come right back to you.

DECEMBER 5

Honesty requires courage.

It takes guts.

To stand in the truth about who we are and who we are not may just be one of the most powerful things we can do.

For outside of honesty and truth we expend huge amounts of energy maintaining veneers and masks that are not accurate.

Nothing is gained.

Honesty and truth rather
will pay you back 100 fold.

New strengths, new
intimacies, new joy, new perspective.

Increase your honesty today.

Thoughts

TAKING ONE DAY / AT A TIME

DECEMBER 6

Compassion is the hallmark of an advanced soul.

Where maturity and graciousness
are front and foremost, we experience compassion.

And where there is compassion, we are changed.

And where we walk in compassion, others are changed.
Put on compassion today.

Better yet, let it invade your soul.

DECEMBER 7

The surest way out
of depression is to do for others.

Taking our focus off of ourselves,
entering into service that puts others
in the forefront . . .

Wow! What a difference this makes.
If your life is stuck, get out there, enter
into something bigger than you,
You will be changed.

Thoughts

DECEMBER 8

To move with the best of times and
with resilience, the worst of times, we
must have soft hearts.

Hearts that are pliable are the only hearts that can
engage in synergy, are good with stretching, and with
resilience find the good even in the midst of the bad.

And hearts that are pliable become so, after hard works
of forgiveness, grieving, and compassion.

Only then are these hearts freed into
solutions, excellence, and grand expectations.

Go for the soft heart. You won't be sorry.

DECEMBER 9

Alongside soft hearts must come firm parameters.

Soft hearts do not mean we are door-mats.
Just the opposite in fact.

(Door-mats must have hard hearts, just to survive.)

Soft hearts, rather, say 'No', hold their spaces,
are good with assertiveness, and are familiar
with intimacy.

Soft hearts know themselves.
Hard hearts are only guessing.

Soft hearts act. Hard hearts are only reacting.

DECEMBER 10

Our external worlds become reordered
when we take the time to reorder our inner world.

The external world merely
gives evidence to what is inside.

This is true of ourselves personally.

It's also true of our businesses and organizations.

This is true of our relationships.
It's also true of our countries and communities.

What is inside us shows up outside.
The fruit is plain to see.

What are we seeing?

What would we like to see?

DECEMBER 11

Becoming intentional creates a shift in everything
we do. Whether it is how we are at home, the
professional goals we have for ourselves, or a
short-term project we want to get done, intentionality
makes all the difference.

A few tips:

> First ask yourself, 'What kind of person do I want
> to be in this?'

> Second, determine, 'What are two new things
> I need to make room for in
> my schedule?'

> Third, 'What are three things I am currently doing,
> that I might set aside for this time?'

With intention comes results. It's just a matter
of setting the space for yourself, committing to
something fresh, and letting some of the old take
a back seat.

DECEMBER 12

During the intense concentration time
of any project there are a few key things
to keep in mind.

One: Make sure you have a good team around you;
   a support system is key.

Two: Focus on the tasks in a disciplined manner;
   doggedly stay on task.

Three: Set small clear goals; set yourself
   up for success.

Four: Speak only what is really happening;
   refuse to tell stories.

Five: Take care of yourself; lead with your strengths.

DECEMBER 13

The surest way to grow and to mature
is to enter into something bigger than ourselves.

In that place all sorts of old lies and coping
mechanisms will come to the foreground.

Giving great opportunity to sort through 'our stuff'.

Contrary to popular opinion this is a grand opportunity.
For we can either stay as we are with life as it is, or we
can grow and have life as it is grow with us.

Go for the growth.

DECEMBER 14

Insecurities hold us back.
They are the great distractions of our lives.

When we are insecure we draw attention
to our own selves in awkward ugly ways.

The solution: head into your insecurity.

That thing you are scared to death to do,
go do that.The fear of this or that, make
that thing part of your life.

Head into your insecurity,
challenge it face-on, and it will diminish.

The supposed big bad monster will step back
and you will be left with a manner of being that
draws no attention to self per se but rather
of confidence and grace.

Thoughts

DECEMBER 15

Listening is one of the most important skills
we must grow. Great listening is never automatic,
rather it is something learned.

Good listening requires that we put our own
biases and paradigms aside, and hear another
just as they are.

Hearing between the lines, listening for emotion,
noticing the unspoken behind the spoken, and paying
attention to body language, are all things that equip
your for great listening.

Practice listening today.

DECEMBER 16

When we are tired or stressed our ability
to speak or listen well reduces dramatically.

Stress reduces our patience level.
It leaves our resilience stretched and thin.

Stress marks our bodies
with illness, and drains our relationships.

Make a plan to reduce your stress.
Your life will thank you.

DECEMBER 17

What might you do today to be ready for tomorrow.

What might you do at this time
to prepare you for your future success.

It doesn't matter what your dreams
or goals are they need some preparation.

Some intention applied.
Some focus given.

Who do you want to be in the world?

Thoughts

DECEMBER 18

The most powerful thing we can do is show up.

Outside of any specific ability
or gifting is the simple goal of showing up.

In the presence of those who take time to give
of themselves we are validated and encouraged.

And simple encouragement is something special,
and in relatively short supply.

Show up, bless on others by simply being there
and you will find satisfaction you never expected.

Showing up - It's really powerful.
Give it a try for yourself.

DECEMBER 19

Every so often it is good
to look at the crops we are planting.

Like every gardener knows
we will harvest what we are sowing.

The seeds put into the gardens of our lives
are the produce we will end up with.

The query - What are we planting, what are we sowing?

Love or hate, trust or suspicion,
generosity or stinginess, hospitality or isolation.

You get the picture. Look deep, examine your ways,
make sure you are really sowing the crop that you
yourself want to have in the end.

DECEMBER 20

What we invest is what we get back.

Wherever we put our focus that is what grows.
The things we track increase.

Make sure you are investing what you want to harvest.
Really know where you want growth and focus on that.

Track only those things you want more of.

DECEMBER 21

We are only as strong, as free,
and as resilient, as the company we keep.

Success leaks out from others to us.

If you want to be more successful
surround yourself with successful people.

DECEMBER 22

Limitations are some of the
most powerful tools available to us.

Perhaps better known as constraint,
when we put limits to our work, to our time,
and to our focus amazing things take place.

What may have taken two months is done in a week.

The energy that would have dribbled away
over time is harnessed for that particular project.

Like a light compressed into a laser beam
the outworking of your goals require some limitation
and constraint to come to best result.

DECEMBER 23

We make big goals and
then we pare it down to the core.

What is the most powerful piece of your expertise?

Do just that thing.

Where will you make the most impact?

Let all other impacts go.

How might you focus your goals?

Prune ruthlessly.
Employ limitation, ensure constraint,
and you will be successful.

DECEMBER 24

Parameters are our best friends.

Learn to manage time
and time will always be there for you.

Ensure money is well tended and it will grow.

Invest in people and people will invest in you.

Thoughts

DECEMBER 25

Courage does any of us a world of good.

If you could take on more
courage today what might that feel like?

How might your life be changed?

What would shift?

Take on more courage today and wear it well.

DECEMBER 26

Between every old thing and every new thing there is a threshold. A space of time and resistance that tests our nerve, demands our best and quite frankly, challenges us beyond what we think we have.

But once past the threshold, entire rooms and new vistas open up to us.

It is here that we find the skills and fortitude learned over the threshold serve us well.

We are stronger, clearer of mind, and convinced of the direction of our days more than ever before.

We are well set to take best advantage of what these new vistas offer us.

DECEMBER 27

Leave complaining at the door.
Shrug off blaming like a bad illness.

Refuse victimhood like the plague.
These things won't do you a lick of good.

In fact, they will take your life down around you.

Rather, shore up your responsibility quotient,
take on the challenges and problems around you,
and allow everything to grow you up and stronger.

Degree by degree this will change your life.

DECEMBER 28

Make mentoring a part of your life.

Look for those to mentor you.
And take it on to mentor another.

Sharing and encouraging others is simply
one of the best ways to be encouraged ourselves.

There is simply little to compare with standing
alongside another's life and seeing growth
and development and go-to-it happening.

Put aside your fears and uncertainties
and take on some mentoring.

DECEMBER 29

Books are some of the best mentors
and manners of learning available to us.

Looking ahead at the year to come, what might
you want to be learning and how might you want
to be inspired?

Think about it.
Make a plan.
Explore the options.

Head to your local bookstore and come
out with what will grow you this next year.

Throughout the year to come,
repeat and repeat some more.

DECEMBER 30

Take a touch of time today and set
yourself down with pen and paper in hand.

In your mind's eye step forward to a year from now.

You have received an A+ for your year.

In a detailed manner write out the exact shifts
and movements of the past year. Take your time,
step into the space of a year from now, and write
about what took place.

Now, tuck what you wrote away somewhere
safe so you can pull it out in a year's time.

You will be amazed!

Thoughts

DECEMBER 31

There is nothing like the
end of a year for taking stock.

A glance back at a year gone by reveals
movements and shifts that we don't notice
in the day to day.

I highly suggest taking a touch of time to make
note of the personal and professional changes that
have taken place over your last year.

You will most likely be pleasantly surprised.

ABOUT THE Author

Born and raised on the west coast of British Columbia, Canada, I've always known and appreciated a great diversity of people.

With five kids of my own, a great son-in-law and a precious grandson life is full and dynamic. An avid reader and a lifetime learner I love all things social media, deeply enjoy gardening and photography, never turn away from a good jigsaw puzzle, and am always ready for a savory bowl of soup and a great cup of tea with a friend.

Find more at **cyndylavoie**.com

For information about publishing with
Capturing Courage Press

publisher@capturingcouragepress.org

CPSIA information can be obtained at www.ICGtesting.com
Printed in the USA
LVOW100603291112

309234LV00005B/22/P